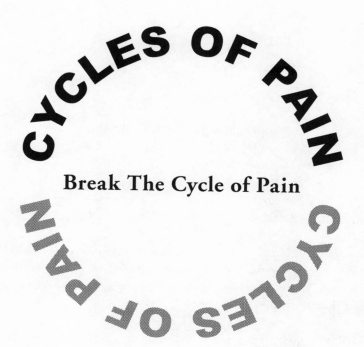

CYCLES OF PAIN

Break The Cycle of Pain

CYCLES OF PAIN

A Book About Overcoming Obstacles
and Living Through Adversity.

Leslie Parker

Library of Congress Control Number:		2016900154
ISBN:	Hardcover	978-1-5144-4017-9
	Softcover	978-1-5144-4018-6
	eBook	978-1-5144-4016-2

insert: Scripture quotations marked NIV are taken from the *Holy Bible, New International Version*®. *NIV*®. Copyright © 1973, 1978, 1984 by International Bible Society. Used by permission of HYPERLINK "http://www.zondervan.com/" Zondervan. All rights reserved. [HYPERLINK "http://www.biblica.com/niv/" Biblica]

Cover design by: Leslie Parker
Photos taken and created by: Leslie Parker

Print information available on the last page.

Rev. date: 03/09/2016

To order additional copies of this book, contact:
Xlibris
1-888-795-4274
www.Xlibris.com
Orders@Xlibris.com
619860

CONTENTS

CYCLES OF PAIN CYCLES OF PAIN CYCLES OF PAIN

CYCLES OF PAIN

To James,

You are a wonderful person & supporter. Thank you so much for supporting me.

Love,
Leslie Parker

Leslie Parker

Dedicate This Book To:

My Father:
Leslie James Jackson, Jr.
I miss his presence and the time that God
allowed me to have with him. R.I.P.

My Grandparents (Father's Side)
Leslie James Jackson, Sr.
Martha Jackson

My Grandparents (Mother's Side)
Ross Leak
Rena Leak

My Grandparents inspired me and taught me how to respect
others and love people despite their imperfections. Also, they
are part of the DNA that made me the woman I am today!

A Special Thanks to My Friends:
Laverne Rollins
Gail Tucker
Donata Mooring
(They pushed me to get my book completed.)

A Special Thanks to My Sisters:
Dawn Jennette
Tamara Jones

In Memory of
Carolyn Fisher: **My best friend**

I never got a chance to say goodbye to her or thank her for her friendship and caring heart. She was like a sister to me!

R.I.P

Ralph Johnson, Jr. (Ronnie)

He was the most compassionate friend I have ever known and he also had a heart of gold. There was something I wanted to tell him, but never got that opportunity to do so.

R.I.P.

ACKNOWLEDGMENTS

I like to dedicate this book to my two beautiful daughters, Nicole and Kelly, who patiently endured the pain and anguish of my torn relationships, and my broken spirit. Yet, they still loved and accepted me even though they encountered some dysfunctional events while growing up. I love them both so much and I am truly blessed to be their mother.

The life I lived was not by choice, but rather by circumstance. I'm just glad I had people in my life that helped me get through this maze! Starting first with God, He placed a hedge of protection around me, even when I did not know him. His merciful love has allowed me to be the woman that I am today. Next is my mother, who gave me the drive and determination to make the best of my life, despite the difficult situations that I encountered. She also kept me going emotionally and spiritually. She gave me the best childhood she knew how and also gave me great direction and guidance. Thank you mom for everything! Then there are my sisters, who are also my best friends. They have played an integral role in my life and are the greatest aunts towards my children and grandchildren. And of course I can't forget my friends who made it possible for me to exhale when I needed to. We all have shared similar experiences and never looked down on each other. When it was time for a safety net to be thrown, it seemed like we all knew when to throw it towards each other. We had our children during the same time, we got married during the same time, some of us separated and divorced our spouses during the same time. So, that's why I want to thank all my friends because we embraced each other over the years and patiently listened to each other when we needed to talk and express our emotions. Last but not least, I want to thank Ernestine Dunston, my Aunt, and Gail Tucker one of my best friends for encouraging me to write this book. I remember when I told that I was writing a book; I shared some of the experiences that I had encountered. These two amazing ladies both were so encouraging when I told them that I wanted to tell my story.

My Aunt is a former school principal and teacher. She is retired now, but has over 35 years of experience in the field of education. I knew that she would be one of the best candidates to choose as my editor. Also, Gail Tucker used to work for The Maryland State Department of Education for over 15 years. Her background in writing is very impressive and solid. That's why I asked her for some advice as well. She is the person who helped me learn how to value myself and my self worth along with my mother and friends.

Again, I have to first give honor to God and give Him all the credit because he selected me as the talking vessel for this book so that others could heal and find refuge! God's words are powerful and especially powerful when you experience them.

INTRODUCTION

It has taken me a little over 30 years to decide to put this book together. Why? I rather tell you about it than explain why it has taken this long to finish something that God has instructed me to do. Before I could even write this book, I had to make sure it was God's will for me to put it together. Now years later after experiencing all kinds of trials and tribulations, I am now able to define my purpose in life, and my will to succeed. I know this sounds crazy, but it's true. I never knew what my purpose in life was until my faith began to be tested. Well, in James 1:2-3 it says, "Consider it all joy, my brethren, when you encounter various trials, knowing that the testing of your faith produces endurance."

My faith was tested in a way that was too hard for me to accept initially. You see, there were **cycles of pain** that took a toll on me over the years; molestation, abortion, abandonment, marriage, divorce, miscarriage, motherhood, abuse, adultery and financial hardships. I know this sound like the typical life that other people encounter, but I believe there was something so different about my experiences, that God gave me a strong conviction and courage to explain these cycles of pain. What I was once ashamed of, no longer had power over me.

Then my life began to have purpose, especially after I decided to release the hurt and pain associated with my experiences. The pain taught me how to love the unlovable, forgive the unforgivable and most of all strive to be the best person that I can be. I always had a passion to be perfect in all my endeavors, and God had to show me how to love myself better and how to understand his love for me. His love is consistent, infallible, understanding, just, empowering, trustworthy and most of all he is faithful.

I was just going through some small storms, and once I realized I found shelter in my life, I started evolving, adapting to change, and rebounding. "The purpose of life is to live a life of purpose", even when life is too complicated to understand. Now brace yourself, this book can be complicated for people who claim to have never experienced a **cycle of pain**. On the other hand, it will enrich the lives of others who may want to tell their stories, but don't know how to express themselves, because of the fear of judgment. Please allow this book to give you some insight to what God is able to do, even in the midst of your storms.

FROM THE BEGINNING

I grew up in a loving family that was poor, but happy! Yes, I was happy! I know it seems impossible for someone to be happy with little resources, but once you learn how to appreciate the smallest things in life, God will show you how to live according to his will.

Now, the person who taught me how to do this is my mother. Let me tell you about this amazing woman before I start to talk about my childhood days. My mother was taught very well by her mother to be a great nurturer, but stern and consistent. That's why her love has permeated from generation to generation.

My mother's name is Clarice and she was born in Liesville, NC along with her three sisters, Martha (oldest), Rena (second oldest) and Sylvania (youngest). Fortunately, her parents took the time to love her and her sisters the way they're supposed to be loved and supported.

From The Top Center: Grandmother
From Left to Right: Aunt Rena and Aunt Martha
Center: My mother (Clarice) at the age of 3 years old.
My Aunt Syl (the youngest) was not born yet.

Now my mother's father was a hard working man. He worked for many years on the railroad. He also had the largest hands I had ever seen in my life.

Whenever he laughed out loud, he would slap you on the back. I don't think he really knew his own strength because when he slapped you on the back it felt like a tree trunk had just hit you. That was his way of saying, "I love you!" And most of the time when my grandfather slapped you on the back, is when he was inebriated. Yes, my grandfather was an alcoholic and drank Sometimes during the week and every Friday & Saturday and was "tore up" from the floor up. However, I never saw him take a drink on Sundays. When he did not drink, he was a total different man. He became somewhat reclusive and would not smile. It did baffle me to see him like that and there were times when I wanted to say, "Daddy Ross everything is going to be okay," but every time I got up the nerve to, I just jumped on his lap and gave him a big hug instead. I knew my grandfather cared and loved me and that is all that mattered to me at the time. He was a man of so much strength and laughter when he was in a good mood. He loved everybody, especially his family. My grandfather gave me the love that I needed during my father's absence. His presence allowed me to feel like I was his little girl and he treated all his grandchildren the same.

He was so much fun to be around! Matter of fact, I used to wait for him when he got off from work. I could see him walking from all the way up the street. He would sway back and forth when he walked and he always had his hat cocked to the side. Back then black men worked so hard to care for their families and I guess drinking was the only way my grandfather could find some release. He probably was going through some emotional, physical, and psychological pain his entire life and he used alcohol to help suppress his pain. He came up in an era where there was horrible racism and black men had a heavy burden on them to keep the family together.

However, I do have some wonderful memories of my grandfather, which I will cherish the rest of my life. I remember being over my Aunt Rena's house when I was 5 years old and this little girl that I played with, said to me, "I know your grandfather" and I replied to her, "No you don't!" My grandfather's tall, he's black, he wears a hat and he's drunk". Wow! Out of the mouths of babes!

My Grandfather: Daddy Ross 1966

Now, my grandmother was a very quiet and meek woman with a great big heart. The heart is where I am today. She would take her last and give it to anybody that was in need. She never said no to my mother or her grandchildren when it came time for needing her assistance. Every Christmas she would give the grand kids the same gift year after year (knitted slippers and stockings for the girls and knitted hats and scarves for the boys). I'm not saying it to be condescending, just to let others know how appreciative I was to get that same gift each year. It was not about the gift, it was about her giving. When she gave you something, it was so heart felt and she never stop showing her love towards her family. She definitely was a phenomenal woman. In case you need further clarification, just read Proverbs 31:10-31 from the bible. She kept my sisters and me in church all day long, both during morning and evening services on Sunday. "I thank you Mama Rena for instilling in me the word of God and a heart of flesh and not of stone." Now, that I've discussed the heart felt feeling about my grandmother, I have to tell you about the funny side of her as well. There was only one issue I had with my grandmother, it was her driving. She could not drive a lick. Whenever we went to church, my grandfather always sat in the back and I sat up front. When they say, "put the petal to the metal," that was my grandmother. She would turn the corner on two wheels and whenever she came to a stop, she would apply the brakes suddenly.

I was scared to death, but never uttered a word. Now, my grandfather use to say, "Rena are you trying to kill me!" Anyway, my grandmother made me laugh so many times.

Now, I need to tell you about my father's parents. My grandmother on my father side was the sweetest woman you ever could have met. She loved her family and her grandchildren just as much. Every Sunday, my grandmother would prepare a nice dinner for her family and her grandchildren. Her cooking reminded me of the dinners that were prepared in the movie "Soul Food." There was always plenty to eat at my grandparents' house. Also, she made the best sweet potato pie I have ever tasted. I called her Mama Martha and some of the other grand kids called her mom. Also, since I was named after my dad, she called me Les. She too was a meek and kind woman. However, she did not take any stuff from anybody. One of my oldest cousins told me that she use to keep a loaded pistol in her bedroom. Occasionally, she would scare my grandfather, Daddy Les (father's dad), with the pistol. Well, it worked, because I never heard my grandfather say anything disrespectful to my Mama Martha. My grandfather Daddy Les was a very quiet religious man and he never raised his voice at his wife, children or grandchildren.

He belonged to the Masons and was in church most of the time. He was born in Black Stock, South Carolina and he was easy to please, as long as he had a hot meal.

The rest of my relatives on my father side are just as caring, especially my aunts, whom I have always admired. They are Aunt Estelle, Aunt Mary Etta, and Aunt Ernestine (all her nieces and nephews call her Aunt Teenie). These three beautiful women are very intelligent, independent and great role models. I have always admired their desire to be well educated and to be go getters. My Aunt Estelle who is the oldest of her sibling has her PHD in Education and is a retired school principal. Her youngest sister, who is my Aunt Teenie, is also a retired school principal, who has two Master Degrees in Education. Then there is my Aunt Mary Etta, who worked for Social Security Disability/Retirement Administration as a Claims Examiner and has a Bachelors Degree in Human & Social Resources. She also has a Theological Degree from Baltimore School of The Bible. My father and his brother Robert Lee were great skilled workers. My father went directly in the Air force after high school and became skilled in electronics. He was the first African American man hired at Bethlehem Steel as an Electronic Assembler and prior to that he worked for many years at MTA (Motor Vehicle Administration) as a Bus Driver. Also, he was a master at crossword puzzles and loved playing cards.

Now his younger brother, Uncle Robert Lee, was an Ammunition Technician at Fort Meade. He graduated from Baltimore School of The Bible and attended Washington College of Religious Studies and was ordained as a minister. He later became a pastor in his own church. He too was a wonderful uncle and pleasant person to be around.

Of course I can't forget about the wonderful aunts on my mother's side of the family. As I mentioned earlier, my mother has three sisters; Aunt Martha (the oldest), Aunt Rena (next to the oldest), and Aunt Syl (the youngest of all the siblings). Aunt Martha reminds me of my Grandmother because of her meek and quiet personality. Always loved to bake and prepare meals for her family. Then there is Aunt Rena, who raised everybody's child in the family (my mothers' kids, my kids, my children's kids, my cousins' kids, her siblings' kids and all the neighborhood children). "In case I did not say thank you enough Aunt Rena, I want to give you your flowers while you can smell them." Thank you for your generous spirit. She is definitely an angel from God! Last but not least, I can't forget my Aunt Syl, my mother's youngest sibling.

She has the "Patience of Job." She's the type of person who will do her best to appease you and make sure your needs are met. She is like a big sister to me. "Thank you again God, for placing wonderful and loving people in my life. Remember love is priceless and even if you're lacking love from a particular person, God will always replace what you're lacking with love!

Now that you have a snapshot of my family, I want to elaborate on my up bringing/childhood experiences.

Meanwhile, moving forward! In 1969, my mother was put into an unexpected situation that forced her to have to raise three girls alone. When this occurred, I was only 8 years old, my sister Dawn was 10, and my oldest sister Tammy was 12. I remember the day just like it was yesterday when my parents separated. My mother was now the head of the household and she worked three jobs to support her family.

She worked fulltime at Bendix as an electronic assembler at night. During the day she worked fulltime as a secretary, Monday thru Friday, and her other fulltime job of course was being a parent. In addition to her work schedule, she maintained two roles at home; mother and father for a very long time! It was not by choice, and unfortunately, my father was busy living his life, because after he and my mom separated, he forgot about the three beautiful girls that God gave him. Not to say that my father did not love my sisters and me, he just did not know how to show his love to us. That's right, God gave him three blessing, that he did not realize was important to him until later on in his life.

This is why I am so compelled to write this novel to perhaps to influence others who may have experienced similar pain, to find comfort in knowing that time will heal their wounded heart. Just remember; **"The heart is deceitful above all things and beyond cure. Who can understand It.?"** (Jeremiah 17:9). Unfortunately, just because you have a parent in your life does not mean you are automatically loved and appreciated. However, God is able to give you what you are lacking in your life!

For example, where my father was lacking as a parent, God made my mother an exceptional loving, and strong minded woman, while raising three girls alone. She is the one who taught me how to overcome obstacles and climb mountains that I never knew I could climb or survive. Don't get me wrong, she is not perfect, but she is consistent. That was the balance, along with God's love that kept me from hitting rock bottom.

Although my dad was not around, my sisters and I still felt loved and cared for, and we did not allow my father's absence to interfere with our day to day life. And thank God, we were still well loved by my father's parents and siblings. We are still blessed today to receive unconditionally love from both sides of our family. Family cohesion is what's lacking in so many broken homes today. Just because you come from a broken home does not mean you should stop communicating with the other side of your family. Take the initiative to draw close to both sides of your family. When you do this, you teach the next generation how to find closure and maintain love towards each other regardless of the circumstances you encounter. I continued to yearn for my father's love, during his absence, but I learned how to suppress those painful moments that I had when I did not see or hear from him. When my mother left my dad, it tore me apart, but again my mother made sure that my sisters and I maintained a close bond with each other and she taught us to be there for each other no matter what the situation was. The tender loving care that I got from my mother and other family members softened the inner pain that I had.

How I wish other parents would do this with their kids. I don't fault my father for not being a good dad. I just wished my father understood the importance of family and fatherhood. Both of his parents were great, especially his mother. She was the pillar and the rock of his family. However, I wish my father would have not been so rebellious and would have listened to the teaching of his God fearing parents. Some men seem to have the proper DNA to be wonderful fathers, but on the other hand there are those men who are very self-centered and complacent with just doing enough.

Lack of commitment to God, will cause a person to seek self satisfaction and have a narcissistic attitude.

Well, I do believe that my father's parents raised my father the best they knew how. I know this sounds contradictory, but apparently, there were **cycles of pain** that existed within his family. Maybe my father was yearning for his father's love, but did not receive it, so he rebelled with his own family. These are all speculations of course. However, these speculations could be the beginning of finding a resolution to slow down the single parent statistics.

Sure life is complicated and if our parents were able to provide us with a road map to follow, we would probably learn to avoid some catastrophic events in our lives. However, the problem is, we spend a great amount of time trying to find the best job, the best house, the best mate, the best look, but we spend very little time getting to know each other, ourselves and most importantly God. If we did we would be able to treat each other with better respect and love.

We tend to chase dreams that are not as important as we think. We also forget that life is just like a vapor, here today and gone tomorrow. That is why we must learn how to live a life of purpose.

If we do not, we will fall victim to depression, oppression and despair. All of this can be avoided if we learn to develop a life project for our lives. Instead, our fears and hurts get the best of us and we rebel against God. I say all of this to tell everyone that you are not alone in your sorrow. So, if you're in pain, it's okay to cry, and to let others know about your pain. We are all still under construction, and are not born perfect. So, stop trying to be perfect for this world. Just try being consistent and perfection will follow.

For example, just imagine how much more powerful the love between my sisters and other broken families would have been if our dads would have loved us unconditionally! Well, despite the efforts of mothers, fathers, and grandparents, children still grow up with pain, resentment, and anger. Not realizing that I myself would one day experience a **cycle of pain**!

This was not supposed to happen to me, a child nurtured and cared for by a wonderful loving mother. Although, my father was absent in the home, my mother was there, so why would I go through changes? One parent is better than none, right? Of course not! It is very important for the other parent to remain in his/her child's life, especially during a child's developmental stages. It is imperative to get reassurance from the absent parent too, because I myself was very angry and resentful towards my mother for leaving my father and I especially resented my father for abandoning my mother, sisters and me. Maybe, that's was why I carried my frustration and resentment towards the men in my life. And to just give you some examples of the resentment, pay close attention to the next chapter.

The memories of my teenage years reflect some mixed emotions; joy, happiness, resentment, pain, anger, rage, hurt and confusion. The list goes on, and it lingered on all the way through my adult life. Until, I finally learned to accept people for who they were and understood that you can not change people. Whenever you deal with difficult people, just remember not to give them your energy or else you will lose yourself and your ability to focus on what is important in your life.

Let me briefly describe my life to you as a little girl. First, I was a joyful and happy little girl until my teenage years. My world changed in the blink of an eye. I became somewhat introverted and afraid, when we had to move from our house on Quantico Avenue to an apartment building on Liberty Heights Avenue. It was a huge 6 unit brick building (with 2 apartments on each floor).

The transition was difficult for me and being poor and black did not give me the option to get family counseling. That was something that was not available for your typical black family during the sixties. So, you just dealt with what you had and made the best of what was available. So, you lived in confusion until you realized that you just had to learn how to adjust to the dysfunctional life that was handed to you. Now, when we moved we met some very nice people in our apartment building. First of all, we lived on the first floor. Next to us was a young couple who had a son. Then on the second level, lived a woman name Ms. Parrot. She had one foster daughter and she worked as a psychiatric nurse fulltime. However, I can't remember who lived next to her.

Now on the third level of the apartment building, was another single woman with three kids. She had two boys and one girl. Next to them was a very nice old lady who lived alone. Her name was Ms. Sutton. I used to visit her everyday just to keep her company. She also had a nephew who would visit her periodically, but still was a very lonely old lady. What I remember most about her was her soft spoken demeanor. She was a very frail white lady who loved to talk and feed you snacks (tuna fish and some of her special desserts). Unfortunately, Ms. Sutton could not cook at all. You know what? Now that I think about it, the food she served my sisters and me, tasted just like cat food! Oh well, it is what it is! I remember when she invited my sisters and me to her apartment for dinner. The food was so horrible, but all we could do was grin at each other and bare it. Because we were raise with kindness and respect, we never insulted her cooking. Also, every time when I would come home, she would be on the third level waiting for me. I had to literally sneak into my apartment without her seeing me. So, to resolve the issue, my sisters and I agreed to take turns keeping her company.

Ms. Sutton also had a pet cat name frisky. When I lived at my house on Quantico, we had a cat and her name was Precious. So, every time I visited Ms. Sutton, I would take every moment to play with Frisky, since he reminded me of my cat Precious. I think the reason we could not bring Precious with us was because my grandmother needed our cat to kill the mice in her house. Plus, the landlord only allowed Ms. Sutton to have a cat because she had been a resident there for awhile. So, little Frisky was grandfathered in!

The landlord was a very nice elderly white man who was friendly towards all the residents in the building. However, he was not the greatest when it came to fixing things in the apartment. Let's just say he took his time repairing important things. For example, we lived on the first floor, but it was a raised level. We had a back porch, which was approximately 10-15 feet off the ground.

The back porch banister was made of wood and was weak. He told my mother and my sisters not to lean against the banister, because he needed to get it repaired. Sometimes, when you're a child, things can go in one ear out the other ear. So, one day my sister Dawn was on the porch tossing a pillow back and forth to her girlfriend Karen. Along side Karen was a neighbor name Nate and me. After the fourth toss, the banister broke and my sister did a somersault in the air three times. It looked like she was attempting a high ski jump and going for the Gold Metal. It seemed like she was in the air forever! We were shocked and stunned. When she finally landed on the ground, she landed on top of the broken banister.

Since we did not know what to do immediately, Nate picked up my sister and took her in the house. He placed her on the bed, but she continued to moan and groan. Believe it or not, we thought if we got her to walk, she would feel better. So, we had her walk back and forth about four blocks to her girlfriend Karen's house and back to our house. Since we were young kids, we did not have any knowledge of how to administer first aid. So, our next door neighbor, Mr. Sam heard the commotion and came over to help. He called the ambulance and later my sister was taken to the hospital. Talk about a close call! We called my mother at work and she rushed home as soon as she could. Also, it seemed like immediately after the accident, a few weeks later, the landlord sold the apartment building. What a coincidence? Perhaps, he wanted to avoid being sued?

Then the following 2-3 months, a very distinguish older black man showed up at the apartment building and introduced himself as the new landlord to the each of the residents. He was a tall fair skinned black man in his early fifties. Having a black landlord during that era was rare. Meanwhile, the landlord became interested in my mother and her girlfriend tried to convince her go out with the new landlord, but my mother was not interested at that time. So, instead of getting involved with the landlord, she dated another male friend, that she met on her job. I believe she was trying to fill a void, but did not know how to stop the pain or hurt herself. Since that relationship was not going the way she anticipated it to go, she did eventually go out on a date with the landlord. Later during their relationship, the landlord offered my mother a job to work part time as a bookkeeper for his oil company.

This part time job enabled her to financially take better care of us. She was able to buy us better clothes and not rely only on hand me downs.

Even when we received hand me downs, we were still appreciative because that was all we had at that time. Then, I started to get perms in my hair and I felt so pretty when my hair was done. Out of all my sisters, I always had the thickest hair and was very tender headed. My confidence increased and I started meeting some very nice friends.

I was glad that I was able to meet some nice friends that I could rely and depend on. As time went by, I started noticing boys and they started noticing me. Well, let me tell you about an embarrassing moment that happened to me. There was this one particular guy who always played basketball at the church courtyard. He started flirting with me. I was tickled pink and was infatuated with him as well. One day I was riding my bike down this steep hill and I noticed that he was looking at me. So, I called myself being cute and I responded to his look by flinging my hair. Then all of a sudden as I was going down the hill, I lost control of my bike and I had to suddenly apply my brakes because I almost ran into a bus. When I applied the hand brakes too fast and too hard, I was thrown off the bike, some 15 feet. In addition, I felled head first with my head sliding across the cement. My hair was long on top and was sliced down to numb after the fall. I laid their unconscious for one minute and then I could hear the guy that I was showing off for, yell from the top of the hill, "Are you okay?" I was in shock, embarrassed and incoherent. So, I grabbed my bike and ran across the street into the apartment building where I lived. The building had a vestibule and I had to ring the door bell just to get in the building. My hair was falling out and it felt like someone had hit me with a sledge hammer and split my head wide open. Finally, my sister Dawn opened the door and just looked at me like I was crazy. She said, "What's the matter with you?" I told her what happen, but I was in too much pain to go into details. Then my older sister comes home and asked my sister, "What dog has been in the building?" "There's a pile of hair all over the place!" When she found out it was mine, she started to chuckle a little and then they both started getting a little concern. They told me to just lie down until the pain goes away. Here we go again; they did not know that you are not supposed to tell someone to lie down immediately after a head injury. Saved by the bell and God! My mother happened to call home minutes after I went into her room to lie down. When my sisters told her what happened to me and that I was sleep on her bed, she immediately told them to wake me up and to call the ambulance. She was on her way home to see about me. Well, I received some x-rays and was examined by the emergency room doctor that evening. He did not see anything that would warrant any alarm, so I went home and rested for a few days.

When I returned to school a week later, I started feeling like I had to pass out. One day when I was waiting for the bus to go home, I suddenly felt like I had to faint. Well, I did faint and when I came to I was on the bus with a bloody nose and lip. It felt like someone had hit me in my face with a shovel. Also, I never saw the person who picked me up off the ground. When I got home, I felt strange and disoriented and nobody was home as usual. My sisters had not gotten home from school yet and my mother was still at work. So, I just waited until my mother called, so that I could tell her about my fainting experience. Well, the mystery fainting experience continued for awhile. So, my mother had to take me to see a specialist and he ordered an EEG (brain wave test). When the results came back, the doctors said that I was fine. Apparently after the wound healed, it must have left a lot of scar tissue.

So, for the next 1-2 years I had intermittent bouts of fainting spells. So, I just learned how to control myself from fainting. I know this sounds funny, but I got tired of fainting in public, so whenever I felt like I had to faint, I would just sit myself down and wait until the fainting feeling would subside.

Meanwhile, my mother contacted my father and told him about my fainting experiences. He did not come around right away, and I started yearning for his attention, so my sisters and I decided to pay a visit to see him the next weekend. Now, I believe the reason why we did not see my father immediately after my parents separated, is because my mother was still angry and hurt by my dad's actions.

She did not disclose this to my sisters and I, why she was so mad, but as time went on I started to figure it out. Apparently, my father became unfaithful to my mother and apparently had several girlfriends throughout their marriage. He had moved into an apartment around the corner from his mother's house and lived above his landlord, Mr. Brown.

Mr. Brown was a nice elderly man, but he did everything possible to protect my father from getting caught! You see, one day my sisters and I caught the bus from the northwest side of Baltimore to the eastside of

Baltimore to visit my father. It was a planned visit and my father knew we were stopping by. His car was outside so we knew he was home. When we arrived, we were so excited to see him. But, when we knocked on the door Mr. Brown came to the door and said that our father was not there. It seemed very suspicious to us.

Then immediately afterwards, a tall light skinned woman, who we had never seen before walked by Mr. Brown and went upstairs to my father's apartment. This left my sisters and I baffled and confused!

Why was our father avoiding us? Well again, things started to look a lot clearer. That woman must have been the new lady in my father's life. Afterwards, we had to get back on the bus to go all the way back home. What a disappointment! If only my father knew how disappointed my sisters and I were. We looked at each other, but did not say a word to each other during the entire bus trip back home.

When we arrived home, my mother looked at us like we were crazy. She said, "Aren't you suppose to be visiting your father?" "And why are you here?" We explained the whole situation to her and boy was she furious. She told us to get into her car and she drove all the way back to my father's house.

That's when all hell broke loose! My mother called my father every name in the book and came out crying. She loved my father so much that you could see the pain on her face when she confronted him and his new girlfriend.

I believe my mother knew about this woman, but hated the fact that my father put a woman before his children. This was a wound that affected my sisters and me for a long time, especially my oldest sister Tammy. She was furious with my father and stayed mad with him for awhile. On the other hand my sister Dawn and I were able to forgive him and overlook his self centered ways.

Tammy is a splitting image of my father. The only difference is that he is dark brown and she is light brown. She very seldom spoke to him until my mother demanded that she respect our father. My mother raised my sisters and me to respect our father, even though he had no respect for us. However, I am glad that we learned how to eventually forgive my father completely. As time went on we learned to give our burdens to God!

Well, forgiving became a hard task to do and took a long time for me to get through all the pain, hurt and disappointment, but yet I persevered!

My mother started to develop a strong relationship with the landlord. That's when she probably needed to suppress her pain. I was happy for my mother, but I still had not accepted this new man in her life. So, occasionally I would have this defiant attitude towards him and did not want him in my mother's life.

Out of all my mother's children, I believe, I was the only one who really had a problem with her new man.

My mother was beginning to show some signs of happiness again. Maybe she decided to release some of the pain she had encountered from her relationship with my father. She had sparks in her eyes that I had not seen in awhile.

Again, I still had this yearning for my father and it was too early for me to even think about calling someone else daddy. Then my mother started taking trips every month with him and I was somewhat jealous of their relationship. Then my sisters and I started going over to my grandparent's house more frequently. You know the old saying, when the cats are away the mice will play. When we got to our grandparents house, we acted like we were so grown.

My grandparents were the funniest couple I ever knew. I really enjoyed being around them and they were very good to my sisters and I. Now, occasionally, my sisters and I would try to pull the wool over our grandparent's eyes. Especially, since we had a little more freedom at their house instead of our own. So, there were times when we would smoke a little pot (Marijuana) and they could never tell. Except for my grandfather Ross! Drunk and all, he would make comments to us about smelling smoke and said that we smelled like reefer! Of course we denied it and just laugh at him. Then, my grandmother would always take up for us and she would say, "Ross, please leave them girls alone." Then they would get into a little argument, but my sweet grandmother would always win.

Grandfather: Ross Leak and Grandmother: Rena Leak

Now, the only thing I did not like about staying at my grandparents' home is when the flying cock roaches came out at night. Whenever I would go downstairs to get something to drink in the middle of the night, I would always have to run to the fridge to avoid having a flying cock roach land on me. I was very terrified of those bugs. Then early in the morning, I would hear my grandmother yelling and banging her broom in the basement. She was trying to kill the rats/mice.

Although, it was terrifying seeing the roaches and hearing rats and mice squeal, I still loved going over to my grandparents' house for some reason. The longest time I stayed with my grandparents is when my mother took a long trip to Europe for thirty days.

It seemed like an eternity to me. My mother's new man swept her off her feet. Love was definitely in the air for her again. Meanwhile, I still had to get adjusted to our new home life and neighborhood and plus I was going through puberty. By the time I reached 13 years of age, things started to evolve in my household.

Life for my sisters and me started to blossom. Our mother got a new job working at General Motors thanks to our next door neighbor, Mr. Sam. He was able to pull some strings to get my mother at GM. We started eating shrimp salad and fish every Friday and my mother started to feel like she was on top of the world. It reminded me of the show "The Jefferson's" because "we were moving on up." Finally, we started living a little life of luxury. However, I still did not feel complete. I don't know what it was, but I had a huge void in my life and my mother's new life with her friend didn't make me feel complete either.

By the time I reached fourteen, I was able to repress a lot of the pain of not having my father around, especially when I started dating. However, it only became a temporary distraction from my inner hurt and abandonment. Meanwhile, my sisters and I used to party like it was 1999 at our house and we partied just about every night. Sometimes my sisters and I would get our older cousins or friends to cop (buy alcoholic beverages) for us, whenever we wanted to get something to drink. Our favorite drinks were, Boones Farm wine, Richards, and Mad Dog 20/20. Well, after I started partying with the older teens, my interest in boys increased.

I will never forget the day when I met the love of my life. He was tall, sexy and handsome. His mother and my mother were childhood friends.

One day my mother stopped by her girlfriend, Ms. Pearline's house. She had three kids like my mother, except she had two boys and a girl. The youngest boy is who I fell in love with. He was sixteen and I was fourteen. When our eyes locked, it was love at first sight. As a matter of fact, the next week my mother went to visit Ms. Pearline and they decided to go to the store, so I opted to stay with Ronnie, my future boyfriend. After they left, a song came on by Minnie Rippleton, "Loving You." Now, I can't sing a lick, but that day, I hit every note by surprise. I guess when love hits; you're able to do anything your heart desires. After I hit the high note, I began rubbing his shoulders and he started singing back to me. We looked like Captain and Tennille or Ashford and Simpson.

By the time our parents came back from the store, we had decided to become a couple. Later during the month, Ronnie asked my mother if he could come by the house to visit me. And of course, my mother said yes since she was good friends with his mother. We got real close as time went on and enjoyed each other immensely. So much that we saw each other every day.

Ronnie was so respectful. He was not a virgin, but I was and he did not pressure me into having sex. Each time we came close to having sex he would always say that I don't have to if I was not ready and I appreciated that about him. However, I started feeling pressure to have sex with him, when my peers told me that they had already experienced intimacy and was wondering what I was waiting for. Plus, I didn't want Ronnie to go anywhere else, so I decided to lose my virginity.

I will never forget the first time we made love; it was so beautiful because Ronnie reassured me that he would not hurt me and that he would always be good to me.

Before we began, he asked me if I was okay and if I wanted to proceed. That was so reassuring! Don't get me wrong, I am not condoning sex at a young age. It's just that I knew that Ronnie loved me and that's what made it beautiful. So, to prevent myself from getting pregnant, I made an appointment with plan parenthood to get some birth control pills.

Meanwhile, my mother started taking more trips out of town and my sisters and I had a ball. We had parties every Friday and of course my boyfriend was over just about every night (she didn't find out about our parties until I confessed to her when I became an adult). When my mother came back from every trip, we made sure that everything was in its proper place and we threw all the evidence on the roof of a detached garage next to our apartment building. We got away with it for a very long time. Except one night, when I got kind of cocky. I had my boyfriend over and we had just finished drinking some wine. We made love and then fell asleep. He tucked me in the bed before leaving, and then I was out like a light. All of a sudden, I heard someone putting their key in the door. With one eye wide opened, I immediately ran down the hall to get to the kitchen. I knew it was my mother and Lord I forgot to do the dishes! One thing for sure, my mother did not play when it came to cleaning her house.

Also, I forgot to discard the evidence! I had a few glasses with the wine in it and I managed to throw the bottles in the trash can, but not on the roof as planned. By the time my mother got to the kitchen I had cleaned up as best as I could, except for this one glass that I missed. My mother use to tell me that she was psychic. During that time I believed her. She decided to pick up this one glass out of all the 12 glassed on the counter. I could see her smelling the one glass from my peripheral vision. So, I started praying and asking God to please not let her open that back door.

The trash can was full of wine and alcohol bottles. I knew that she was going to open the door once she asked me, "Why are you still up?" Sure enough, she opened the door and came back inside with three bottles in her hand. She began to back me in the corner of the pantry, which also had a window in it. I felt like a rat being cornered. She asked me, "Where did the bottles come from? Of course my immediate response was a lie. I told her that my cousin Noonie stop by with a few of his friends. She called my bluff and said that she was going to call Noonie to verify the information.

So, I pleaded with her not to call Noonie and told her another lie. I told her that the bottles belonged to my cousins, Michael and Bryant! By then my mother's patience grew thin and I finally confessed and told her the truth. The truth does not set you free all the time because after I confessed, she chased me around the dinning room table about five times and swung at me a couple of times. I felt like I was in the ring with Mohammad Ali and was doing the rope a dope!

Then she chased me down the hall to the bathroom. We had a very long hall. Thank goodness because I was able to lock myself in the bathroom for a short while. Then she started banging on the door with the broom. At this time, I'm saying to myself, "Is this woman crazy?"

She used reversed psychology on me and told me that she just wanted to talk to me and that she was not going to beat me. Because I trusted her, I decided to unlock the bathroom door. I slowly came out and found her sitting on my sisters' bed, telling me to come and sit beside her. She said that she just wanted to talk to me. Oh what a fool I was? As soon as I sat down beside her, she gave me the whipping of a lifetime and afterwards, she had the audacity to tell me that it hurt her worse than it hurt me? Yeah right! What planet is she from?

After that ordeal, I did straighten up for a little while, but I still thought I was grown and started to really smell myself. I was more careful not to leave alcohol around and I continued to be with my boyfriend and party every night like a rock star. Don't get me wrong, I feared my mother's wrath, but I still felt like I could do what ever I wanted to do.

My father was not there to discipline me and my mother was working nine-ten hours a night. My sisters were doing their thing and I had so much free time on my hands that it could have killed me. Well, the next chapter will reveal how having so much free time, can be dangerous.

VIOLATED AND SCARED

Life seemed to be going well with me, my new love and my new feeling of euphoria! However, things took a turn for the worst a year later. I befriended a girl, who lived two houses down from me. She had a little brother and she lived with her mother. Her mother was also a single parent who had to work long hours just to support her family too. She also had relative who stayed with them occasionally, whenever her mother had to work late.

As the months went by, she and I became very close. One day I stopped past her house and her relative opened the door. I asked for my friend, but he said, "Oh sweetheart she isn't here, she's at my other sister's house." "Do you want me to take you there?" I didn't hesitate to say yes, because I thought I could trust him and it was not like I just met him. So, I decided to let him take me to see her.

My mother always worked at night; therefore I was able to get out when I felt like it. Oh believe me; I knew to be back at a respectful time. Well, that is when the saga began, I accepted a ride with him to go and get my friend.

It seemed like he was driving for a long period of time and I asked him, "How much further do you have to go? He said, "We're almost there I just have to make one quick stop at my house." His house was located in Baltimore County. Now, keep in mind, I lived in the Baltimore City, which is approximately twenty-five minutes from Baltimore County in Maryland. I didn't know that at the time, not until I got older. He stopped past his house and had me wait outside.

Suddenly, he came out his house and motioned for me to come in. He said that he left his food out on the stove and didn't want it to go bad. As if he was explaining the reason for his detour. He offered me something to eat. So, I thought that he was just being very hospitable since I knew his niece and I thought it was okay to be there.

Was I ever wrong! Minutes later, he offered me some food and then poured me a glass of wine to have with my food. At first I declined, but he was so convincing that he persuaded me to take the drink. Taking the drink made me feel like a woman. Besides, my mother would never find out that I had a glass of wine. What's the big deal, it's only wine? Well, it wasn't only wine. As soon as I took a few sips of the wine, my body literally went limp.

Next, I started to lose my vision and then I felt my body being raised in the air. He raised me in the air and carried me like a baby to his bedroom. Still in shock and incoherent, I didn't know what to expect. I could not scream or talk during this ordeal. But I do have vivid memories of what he did to me. The very next morning, I felt strange, filthy and upset. Asking myself questions like: Did my friend's relative rape/molest me? What happened to me? How did I get home? I never told a soul and decided to keep this from everyone I knew!

Two-Three months went by and I tried to live my life as normal as possible, but it was hard living this horrible secret. Fortunately I was involved in the dance program at my high school and my passion was to become a professional choreographer, like Alvin Ailey and Martha Graham. This love for dance kept me sane and helped me repress the pain. By the time the fourth month rolled around, my life started to change drastically.

I did not have a period, so I assumed that my body was just going through some changes. Not realizing that I was pregnant, not by Ronnie but by the man that raped me, my girlfriend's relative. The reason why I knew it had to be from him is because Ronnie and I were very careful and we used protection. Plus, immediately after I was molested I did not want to have intercourse for a while.

I was very fit and had a nice body, because of my professional dancing. Therefore, my stomach never got big and I didn't think pregnancy at first. Well by the fourth month my stomach started getting big and one of friends from school made a remark about my stomach. She said, "Why is your stomach so big?"

I told her that I had been just eating a lot. However, I knew something was not right and that I needed to let my mother know that I had not seen my period for awhile. So, I decided to tell her that I had not seen my period for 3-4 months. Afterwards, I asked my mother, "What was happening to me?" Of course she went crazy and became upset with me. She immediately called the doctor to schedule an appointment for me to be seen. Also, she assumed that I had gotten pregnant by Ronnie.

Looking back, I realize my mother did what she felt would be best for her little girl and I'm sure she did not want me to experience the same hurts she had experience as a single parent.

I had very mixed emotions about having an abortion and I felt like running away. Dear God? What was happening to me? Can I go forward after this? Well, I did manage to regroup physically, but I still was an emotional wreck internally. Right afterwards, I got better and I resumed my dancing. Thanks to God and dance, which I ultimately believe saved my life, kept me sane, and allowed me to heal for a short while.

Ronnie and I continued our relationship and grew closer. The very next year, our sex life increased and for some reason I started having unprotected sex. The real situation was never addressed, and more **cycles of pain** just followed. And I got pregnant a few more times, this time by Ronnie and I felt like I had the right to make this decision on my own without my mother's consent. I know it sounds like I had a license to kill, but I really did not know what to do. I feared my mother and my relationship with Ronnie started going south.

We started drifting apart by the time I turned seventeen. Ronnie could no longer deal with the pain or my immaturity. He started working more hours and ironically after he stopped by to see me, he started receiving phone pages from everywhere, including from an older woman. His behavior started changing towards more and I started seeing less of him. His excuse was that he had some emergency calls that he had to take care of. Also, during that time he worked at an apartment building as the Heating & A/C Supervisor and starting driving a white car that I never seen before.

The signs were written on the wall and we were slowly but surely breaking up with each other. By the time I got to my senior year of school, I was really involved in dance, since it was my major in school.

TRAGIC YEAR

1979 was my senior year in school and a very tragic year for me! I am surprised I did not lose my mind. Starting with Ronnie, he continued to show signs that he wanted to break-up with me. He purposely started an argument, so that he would not have to take me to my senior prom. The week before my prom, he told me that he was not going. Oh! I was so furious with him, yet I still tried to get him to take me.

Then one evening, my best girlfriend Carolyn called me and said that that she needed to talk to me about something. Apparently, she was going through some changes herself and wanted to talk to me about her pain.

Unfortunately, when she called me, I was too busy trying to get Ronnie to change his mind about the prom and I was being very self-centered at that time. So, when she called I told her that I would call her back. Of course my mind was on myself at the time and not on my friend who really needed to talk to me.

The next day came and I got fitted for my gown that my sister had sewn for me. It was lavender and was made from a Vogue pattern.

Meanwhile, I was still in limbo with whom I was taking to my prom since Ronnie was being very evasive and difficult at the time. I completely forgot about calling Carolyn back that evening and the next day.

So on the second day, when I was standing in the line for lunch, I over heard a few people talk about a tragic accident that happened the night before. A girl was hit by a tractor trailer and her body was thrown several feet in the air. I tried to ease drop, but all of a sudden my heart got real heavy, and I no longer wanted to hear their conversation. Then suddenly, one of the girls turned to me and said, "You know her!" I looked at her like she was speaking a foreign language.

She repeated her statement again, this time with further description. "You know her!" "You guys used to hang together everyday at Greenspring Middle and Garrison Middle." By this time, I was numb and in shock! Then another girl said, "Yeah, the girl that died was Carolyn Fisher!" Oh my God! Oh my God! Jesus help me! That was all that came out of my mouth! I immediately dropped my tray and ran down the hall to my dance studio looking for my dance teacher, Ms. Beverley Johnson. When I found her, she was in the dance studio by herself.

So, I immediately ran up to her, clenching onto her for dear life. I felt like I had just fallen out of a plane and was falling to my death. It also felt like all the air was removed from my lungs and airways. I could not get my breath and it seemed like it took me hours to tell her why I was crying. Finally after having my teacher hug me and console me, I was able to tell her that I just found out that one of my best friends was tragically killed in an automobile accident. She comforted me the best she knew how. Then she immediately put on some soothing music to calm me down. Afterwards, she told me to just dance and express my hurt and pain through movement. She later explained to me that "music and dance is therapy for the soul." I can attest to that today.

I could not stop crying because I felt so guilty that I did not have a chance to talk to Carolyn and she was taken from me so soon. Why did I put myself before her? What was she trying to tell me? These were the questions I had on my mind. I lived with this guilt for a very long time. I still get emotional sometimes when I think about it. To add more sorrow to the situation, her boyfriend was in the Army and he was on his way home from North Carolina to take her to her prom the next day or two.

Carolyn's death took place on I-70 in Columbia, Maryland. She was on her way to Columbia Mall with a few other girls to pick-up their prom dresses. The car that she was riding in had experienced some car trouble and the driver of the vehicle had to pull on the shoulder of the road. Meanwhile, a tractor trailer truck driver missed his turn and at the last minute swerved his rig right into the path of the car that my girlfriend was standing by.

During that time, nobody was in the vehicle. However, Carolyn and her friends were all standing near the car, including a Good Samaritan who had stopped to offer the girls assistance with their car. When the truck driver swerved his rig at a high rate of speed, the other girls stayed closed to the disabled vehicle, but Carolyn and the Good Samaritan ran and Carolyn was struck in the face/temple of the truck's right mirror (according to her sister and boyfriend). The impact threw her into a large tree and by the time the paramedics came to work on her, she was gone. Also, I understand the guy that helped her was killed and died immediately on impact as well.

CAROLYN'S FUNERAL

The day of the funeral was the longest and most sorrowful day of my life. The funeral was packed with young kids from every school; Greenspring Middle, Garrison Middle, Walbrook Senior High, and Western High School (which is an all girl school where Carolyn attended). Her mother, step-father (her real father died when she was a baby), sister and her little brother, were sitting on the first row! They were starring at Carolyn's casket like it was a bad dream.

It took everything I had to approach her casket. And when I did, I could not let go of her. I could not believe she was gone and could not bare anymore pain. So, when the funeral was over, I decided not to go to the cemetery and have never been there since she died.

Also, after the funeral, I went home to finish mourning. Ronnie called me and decided to come over to console me that evening, but I could tell that he was no longer with me emotionally.

My heart grew heavier each day and I cried everyday. I started talking to my sister about the Lord and how could I have a relationship with him, because this burden was too hard for me to handle. My sister Dawn found Christ at the age of 12 and used to try to get me to visit her church in the past.

Well, she no longer had to convince me what I needed. It was a wakeup call for me and I knew it was time for me to ask God to come into my life! I started going to church with my sister and her girlfriend Karen. The church was a holy evangelistic church. Where they spoke in tongues and ran up and down the aisle. When I first attended, I just watched and listen. Then it only took about 2-3 Sundays before I experienced God's love and humility in my life. I remember the day just like it was yesterday. I proceeded down the aisle when her pastor asked, "If anyone out there wanted a relationship with God?" I began to feel the Holy Spirit take over my body as soon as I asked God to come into my life and my heart. I have to explain to you what it felt like to have this life changing experience take place. First of all, when I tilted my head back, tears started rolling down the side of my face uncontrollably, and then my body felt like it was being raised in the air.

Immediately afterwards, I started talking in tongues, a language that I had never spoke before. Then I felt a strong comforting feeling come over my entire body. It was as if my natural father was holding me and telling me that everything was going to be all right. I had an outer body experience and an inner body change.

Although I was still mourning my girlfriend's death, I had an overwhelming feeling of comfort, peace, and serenity. It was the greatest high that I had ever experience. Yet, my flesh became week in months to follow.

COLLEGE LIFE

Meanwhile as months passed by, I tried to live my life holy and acceptable in God's sight, but as time went by I started back sliding once I started attending college. I attended Morgan State in September 1979 and was amazed with college life.

I began to meet new friends and new guys. The guys during that time were very nice and respectful. Now, my first year at school was an adjustment and I still continued to dance. I had taken an advance modern dance class so that I could keep up with my skills and to keep myself emotionally grounded. I changed my major to Broadcasting (Directing for Television). Morgan State is Morgan State University now.

My sister Dawn was already attending Morgan State and her major was Business Administration. What was nice about it was that we both were in the same speech class, one semester. And because we look so much alike, people knew immediately that we were sisters.

Dawn eventually graduated from Morgan with high honors because she was always a pretty focused student. She never allowed anybody to interfere with her studies. I, on the other hand, was still struggling with self. So, I would always fall in love or somehow get distracted.

**Dawn, My Father and Me at my father's place
(Dawn's Graduation)**

As the storms of life were ranging, I needed to find some inner peace and comfort as well. However, that was not happening for me right away, because my grandfather had lost his battle with cancer.

I remember when the family arrived at the hospital. When the doctor came out of the operating room, he shook his head and told my grandmother, my mother and my aunts, that he was not able to remove the cancer. It had spread thru his whole body. So instead of getting my grandfather upset, my grandmother told my grandfather that most of the cancer had been removed. My grandfather had just retired from working at the railroad company for 30 years! What a way to live your life. Work all your life and as soon as you try to enjoy it, it's gone in a blink of an eye. That's why I emphasized to "Live The Life That You Love and Love The Life That You Live!" My grandfather died in December 1979.

Oh I cried like a baby! I missed my grandfather so much. He was a strong man who loved his family and worked like a dog to provide for his wife, children and grandchildren.

Then the following year, September 1980, is when I really lost my focus. I took a German class and set next to this fine guy name D.J. The reason I am using his initials is because this guy hurt me so bad. I did not think that I could hurt any worst than I did when Ronnie and I broke up. Well, D.J. was about three-four years older than me. He was very suave and debonair. I was attracted to his smile and his wit. He was a sergeant in the army reserves and was a very intelligent man. I admired his personality and demeanor. The attraction between us began immediately and he could speak German fluently since he was previously in the service. Anyway, I had a strong attraction for this man.

He volunteered to help me with my German and suggested that we study together. Of course I accepted and then the roller coaster ride began. My nose was so wide open that I would forget to call home and let my mother know where I was.

You know that old saying, "You reap what you sow." What happened to me next was no one's fault but my own. I started becoming defiant towards my mother. She specifically told me to at least call her if I was not coming home. Of course being grown, I did not give my mother the courtesy of a phone call. I stayed over at D.J's house just about every weekend. When we went on our winter break, I stayed over his house from December 25, 1980 thru January 15, 1981. I literally lost my emotional mind!

My mother had no idea where I was, except that I was with my new boyfriend. She did see signs of me coming home because my room looked like someone had been in the room to get clothes. And of course, I did leave a note. However, I was too scared to call her so I just waited until January 16, 1981 to come home. Well, the day before I came home, D.J and I decided to attend the march in D.C. The purpose of the march was to make Martin Luther King's birthday a national holiday. We marched for a long time and I did not have the proper shoes on. I had on these beige canvass shoes with no insulation. What in the world was wrong with me? I guess I was just being a teenager. Well, later that evening I got sick. The soles of my feet were so pale and white and I could not feel my toes. All of a sudden, I started trembling and shaking, so D.J. ran a hot tub of water for me and put me to bed. Afterwards, we made love!

Once I arrived at my house, my mother was sitting in the kitchen and she had this look of disgust on her face. I know she wanted to knock me out, but she didn't, thank God! She let me get settled in and told me to come see her afterwards. Well, I tried to drag the time as long as I could.

When I finally sat down to have a talk with her, she scolded me and asked me when was I going to learn and how could I be so inconsiderate? Now back then it was no big deal, but ask me the same question now, I'm sure I would have answered it differently.

You will never believe what happened a few weeks later. I had that worse flu like symptoms: I had body acnes, I could not keep my food down and I started losing weight. Could I be pregnant I asked myself?

Well over the next two weeks I tossed and turned with the decision to have another **abortion!** God was speaking to my spirit and I was at a tug of war with my flesh. My flesh was seeking instant gratification, but my soul was crying out to God!

On the morning that I was scheduled to move forward with the abortion, is when my sister Dawn came from no where, and wanted to talk to me. She asked me if I was okay and if I had something on my mind. It reminded of the bible, when Nathan, came to David about a dream he had. Well, my sister was like Nathan and she elaborated that God told her to speak to me about a decision that I had to make.

My first response to her was no! Then later on that day, the Holy Spirit told me to tell her what my plans were. Talk about divine intervention. So, I opened up to Dawn and told her what was going on with me and begged her not to tell our mother. I told her that I was scheduled to have the abortion that day. She pleaded with me not to go through with it and simply told me don't do anything that I would regret later on in life.

It was as if God had my life on film and was rewinding it to show me all the abortions and the babies that came from my wound. So, I began to sob and I told my sister that I was afraid and that I did not want to upset our mother. Well, she gave me the courage to approach my mother later that day and tell her my situation. So, when my mother came home from worked, I told her that I needed to talk to her and she asked me out of the blue; Are you pregnant? I was in shock and asked her, "What makes you think that I am pregnant?" Then she asked me again! "Are you pregnant?"

When I replied, it was like I was talking in slow motion. I said, "Yes I am pregnant!" "How did you know?" She told me that I showed all the symptoms of being pregnant and that she just had a feeling. Talk about a mother's intuition! After our talk, she said, "Whatever your decision is I will support you." However, she told me that when you make your bed hard, you have to lie in it. She also said that she would help me, but I had to be responsible. Then she asked me about D.J. and if he was going to do the right thing. I told her with confidence that I did not foresee any problems.

EMOTIONALLY WOUNDED

The very next day, D.J. called me and I told him that I decided not to go through with the abortion and that I wanted to keep the baby. He did a 180 degree turn on me when I told him that I was keeping the baby. All I could think of at that time was: Oh what tangle webs we weave! I went back and forth with D.J. over my decision and he fought me on it for days. Then he made a statement that blew my mind: He said, "I know you are trying to trap me and I am not getting married." I responded to him and let him know that I was not trying to trap him, but that I wanted to do the right thing in God's sight.

He did not know my story, so I did not volunteer to tell him. He probably would not have cared anyway! He later began to ignore me when he would see me in the school hallway and then to add insult to injury, he started dating this new girl a few months later. Of course this made me very distraught, but I continued to hold my head up high! I asked God to please help me get through this **painful cycle**!

The remaining months of my pregnancy was a joy! I had a tremendous amount of support from my friends, relatives and strangers.

So, I managed to blossom and keep my faith. After class, I would always stop past my Aunt Rena's house and would eat so much until I fell asleep. I also traveled with my mother a lot, going back and forth to Boston or down south to visit my great aunts. Believe it or not I learned how to repress the abandonment pain that I had experience. It was as if I got pregnant without a man. I continued to love life and allow life to love me. I did however gain a lot of weight during my pregnancy. I went from a mere 115 lbs to 175 lbs.

On September 15, 1981 I had a doctor's appointment to get weighed in and to listen to the baby's heart beat. Also, I was a few days over my due date, so my doctor decided to induce labor, by breaking my water.

She explained to me that in a few hours I would start to feel some uncomfortable contractions. She also said that if my contractions got worse, to give her a call. Well, they did and I called her later that evening.

My regular doctor was not available that day. I believe he was out of town, so I had a woman doctor from Germany, who talked me into having my baby naturally! What in the world was I thinking?

I thought that I was doing an honorable thing by not taking any drugs or medication to relieve the pain. Was I ever so wrong! What was I thinking? Two to three hours after she broke my water, I began to have some very strong contractions.

Then I started to have some strong pains in my lower back. I could not get comfortable and I tossed and turned for hours. The labor pains started at 5:00pm on Sept 15, 1981 and ended on September 16, 1981. That is when I delivered a beautiful daughter, 8lbs 5 ounces. I pushed so hard that my eyes felt like they were popping out of my head. Do you know that after my daughter came out, all the pain that I had experienced dissipated? My mother was in the delivery room with me and that was so reassuring, compared to my ordeal five years ago! The very first thing I said to her was, "Did I do that (just like Erkle use to say on the Family Matters show)?" Child bearing is amazing and it is a blessing. And most of all, I thank God for allowing me to experience motherhood.

I had to stay in the hospital for a few days and I was in a lot of pain the next day. The doctor gave me an episiotomy during the delivery and that's when they cut you from the end of your vagina to the beginning of your rectum! Then they stitch it up! Because of the numbing medication, you don't feel anything until the next day.

Well, it hurt so bad that I was afraid to have a bowel movement. It felt like I was split open all over again!

When I arrived at home from the hospital with my new baby girl, I started feeling like I was in a fog. I begin crying inside and out loud. The strangest thing is that I was happy but scared. When I went to lie down, I took a long look at my daughter and asked myself, "How am I going to raise you? And what is the future going to be for me as a single parent?"

Suddenly, I started reflecting on how my mother miraculously raised three little girls with God's help. I am sure it would be okay for me too! This was my way of convincing myself that it was not as bad as it seem. Also, to have faith in my Lord and Savior Jesus Christ!

Later that evening I snapped out of the fog and began receiving guests throughout the day! People started coming out of the woodwork to see my baby girl. So, after my guest left, I started to appreciate my blessing more than ever. I knew that God would be in my corner no matter what the situation looked like! I did have a job while I was pregnant. So, earning money was not a problem for me then. Also, my employer allowed me to be off for at least 3 months.

He said that I would still have my job once I return to the work. That was so reassuring.

Well. I called D.J. the next day to tell him about our beautiful daughter, but he never returned my call. Then I managed to get his parents number who lived in Georgia at the time. When I called his parents' home, his mother answered the phone and I properly introduced myself to her. I continued to talk to her about her son and how our relationship started.

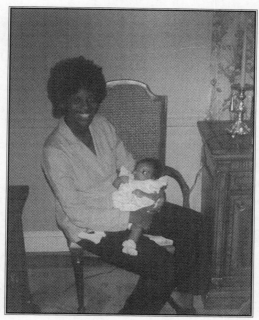

Me and my new baby girl:
Nicole: Sept. 1981

Once I could tell that she was a pleasant person to talk with, I told her that I just delivered a baby girl a few weeks ago and I asked her if her son told her about the new grandchild that was coming.

Everything went silent. Her personality changed as fast as lighting. She no longer had a warm conversation with me. Don't get me wrong, I know it probably was a shock to her, especially since she never met me before. So, I tried to give her the benefit of the doubt. However, she never took the initiative to find out what was going on. As the months went by, she never tried to get in contact with me or even make an attempt to come see her granddaughter. This really crushed my spirit and my heart. How can people be so insensitive and cruel?

This meant that Nicole would never meet her father's side of the family because of this type of behavior. Unfortunately, this happens all the time. What is wrong with this world? How can people deny what is a part of them. God is not happy with the way we treat each other and father's need to step up to the plate. Men and women, just because you don't want a relationship with each other anymore does not mean you have the right to reject your own child.

Well, I had no choice but to continue on with my life and from that point; I just tried to make the best out of my situation as possible.

There's an old saying, "You can't make somebody love you or care for you!" So, I just acted like they never existed. Now, I knew that eventually my daughter would ask me about her father, so I had already prepared myself in advance for those questions. I had to concentrate on what was happening at that time. Basically, I had to learn how to live one day at a time.

Fortunately, I have a wonderful family and strong support system. In addition, my supervisor was a very friendly and understanding employer. He re-arranged my work schedule, so that it would accommodate my family life with my new born child. Now, my supervisor was a family man but deep down inside he was an unhappy man. He would come to work intoxicated and depressed. But every time, I needed to take off to take care of my daughter, he would grant me the time off without question. **Thank you God again for another blessing!** Not only did my supervisor give me the time off I needed, he promoted me to Assistant Manager, of the Check Cashing Company. Although I worked long hours there, I really enjoyed my job because I felt appreciated.

I come from a family that believed in order to succeed you should stay on a job forever. That was not my belief! I am too adventurous to stay at one job for a lifetime. Plus, I truly believe that God's plan for my life required me to be a mentor and talking vessel for him. However, my mother would often criticize me for hopping from job to job.

She did not realize that I was too creative to stay at one job forever. It was not in God's plan for my life. Now, I am not knocking anybody who wants to stay on a job forever. I think that's great, but like Jay-Z said in one of his songs; "It's Not For Everybody." So, there! For some reason, I knew that God had a unique plan for my life, despite the trials and tribulations I had encountered.

As time went by, I started craving for my independence and told my mother that I wanted to get my own place. She just looked at me and smiled. She told me that I didn't have a pot to piss in or a window to throw it out. She always would use little clichés or analogies, when she wanted to make a point. A few months later, I did move with my cousin and guess how far I went?

I moved directly cross the street from my mother's house. I would stop by her house to get food because after I paid my rent and daycare, I had no extra money for food. Mom was right! I could not even afford the rent where I stayed.

It was not that it was expensive I just did not have enough income to afford all the expenses with my little salary and with a child. Well, I only stayed in my new place for 6 months. I had to swallow my pride and move back with my mother. She only asked me to pay her $100 a month for rent. But at that time, I thought she was not being fair. Well, after being out there for a little while made me realize how fair and supportive she really was.

JOY AND PAIN

On September 16, 1982, my baby girl turned a year old and I had her birthday party at my cousin's house. Since the weather was so nice, I decided to have it outdoors. It was a lovely day that day and of course Nicole's father was not present that day. I know I sound bitter and I guess I was somewhat. Here we go again, the **cycle of pain** and how it repeats itself. Nicole's father was not in her life and all I could think about was how it would affect her in the future. She was happy and did not even know that her father existed, so why should I feel bad. Well I did, but I learned to make the best out of a bad situation.

As the day went by, my mother was at the party and I walked inside to find her on the phone looking very concerned and distraught. When my mother got off the phone, I asked her who she was talking to. She said that it was my oldest sister's husband. He told my mother that my sister was in critical condition. She was involved in a terrible car accident, while she was stationed in Texas. He did not give my mother all the details, except that it was imperative for my mother to get to Texas as soon as possible.

**Nicole's First Birthday Party,
Sept. 16, 1982**

Well, I continued to try to celebrate Nicole's birthday the best I could, but it was hard. So, we had to end the party sooner than expected. My mother called several people in our family, both on her side and my father's side. Then later that evening she managed to get a flight out to Texas the very next evening. I could not go at that time, because I had to stay home and take care of Nicole. Plus, I could not afford the plane fare. However, my mother, father, and my grandmother on my father's side flew to Texas to provide support to my sister and her husband. Her injuries were pretty bad. According to my mother, my sister was driving along a two lane road, when she suddenly saw this bright light, and that was all she could remember. But according to a witness, my sister was ejected out of her car while falling down a huge embankment. The car flipped over several times and almost landed on top of my sister. By the time the car made its last flip, my sister who was lying flat on the ground, body was miraculously raised straight up and rested on the vehicle.

As I mentioned before, she sustained some bad injuries; a broken neck, a back injury and her left arm was damaged pretty badly and the whites of her eyes were completely dark red. The sad thing about her injuries was that she almost did not make it. She was stationed in the military and was rushed to a military hospital for care. The medical staff had her up walking, to later find out that her neck was broken. In addition, her left arm was broken and had a severe gnash on it. The military hospital staff at Fort Hood, Texas, placed a cast on an open wound, which almost caused gangrene to set in.

There were other complications, but fortunately she was able to come home to heal after being in the hospital for a few months. When she came home she had on an upper body cast with a metal halo screwed in her head to support her broken neck. She was very depressed and distraught and did not want to live. She was in so much pain and was totally dependant on her husband to bath her.

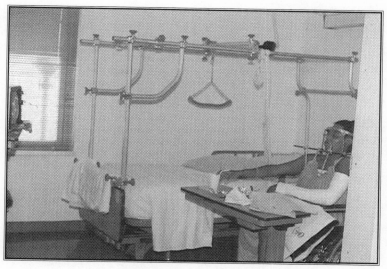

Tammy in the hospital in Texas

Why does things like this happen to people we love? Only God knows. Thank God my sister was able to make a full recovery. It took some time for her to turn her neck or move it at a certain angle. Do you know that during that time, my father became so distraught after my sister's accident? He started to appreciate us better than before. "All things work together for good." Maybe that explains why this incident had to happen. It brought us closer to each other.

So, the next time you encounter a tragic moment in your life, know that God will never leave you comfortless or alone. Tammy was able to get back on her feet after months of therapy. She got a job working in the hospital and she soon was promoted to supervisor of her department. She and her husband lived on the second floor of my mother's house and she eventually was able to get back to herself again.

THE DATING GAME

I few years later, I started dating again and this time I met an older man just like my mother. When I met him, he told me that he was only 34, and at that time I was approximately 22 years old. At first, I was uncomfortable with the age gap, but as time went by I became quite comfortable, because he made me feel like a woman. He was such a gentleman and he was good to me. He paid my rent, bought me a car and I never had to spend a dime when we went out. Now, when we met he told me that he was married, but separated and was in the process of getting his divorce. I believed him because we were together just about everyday.

We dated for two years and then the bombshell came. One day I was visiting a friend of the family in the hospital. Who had just given birth and within a few minutes later, I received a page from my little cousin Michelle. Michelle was 16 years old at that time. She left me a message to call her as soon as possible.

So, I asked the friend of the family if I could use her phone. She said, "Sure." So, when I called my cousin to find out what was the emergency! She asked me if I was sitting down.

She said she asked her boyfriend if his father still lived there and he said yeah, but that his parents were going through a separation. The man I was dating was her boyfriend's father. Here I go again, another **cycle of pain**. This time it was mistrust and anger all in one. Later that day I approached my friend and asked him to come over because I needed to talked to him about something important.

Well, I did forgive him for a short while, but I lost that trust with him, so I started dating someone else six months later. This time it was with a co-worker of mine. He was about four years older than me and he just finished school at the University of Maryland, College Park. He was studying to be an attorney.

I started becoming attracted to him, after I trained him. He was being trained to run another check cashing store and I was his supervisor.

Later that evening when we closed the store, I agreed to give him a ride home since his car was in the shop. However, by the time we approached my car, I had a flat tire. So, he had to change the tire and it was pouring down raining at the time.

Watching him change the tire in the rain was very sexy to me, and I started watching his every movement from head to toe. We began to talk about everything. We talked about my goals, his goals, and whether or not I was in a relationship. Since he asked me first, I asked him the same question. I definitely did not want to get into another relationship with a married man.

A few months went by and then I decided to date him. When he moved to his new store to work, it made it better and easier for us to date. The only person within the company that knew we were dating was his aunt. She was a manager at another store location. I later began to meet his parents and siblings. He came from a family of all boys.

Once I met everyone from his family, they welcomed me and my daughter. We felt like we were part of the family.

My confidence started to grow and I had a great guy in my life. Unfortunately, I was still a little immature and did not understand why my new man was always working even after work. He was the President of his neighborhood association plus he would get together with his former college friends from time to time. I started to feel a little jealous and needy, especially, when he did not invite me to one of the functions with his former college friends. I totally reacted like a child. Tony and I started having little fights and I refused to let him boss me around! I became this strong willed person after awhile. I think it was because I was a little jealous of his success and wished I had finished college myself during that time. Well, Tony and I continued to date and he asked me to be patient with him.

He was also responsible for a several organizations that he formed and he said that he wanted to marry me. I was the one that was impatient. I remember one particular weekend when we got into an argument over money and going out. He decided to hangout with his friends, so I went out with my friends that evening. Well, later on that evening I got a call from my ex-boyfriend Richard. He said that he would like to see me. Remember, this man spoiled me like I was his daughter. So, because of the flesh, and greed I got weak! I became very materialistic and wanted to be with someone who would provide for me now and not later. So, later that evening I invited Richard to come over.

He stayed with me all that night and the next day! That was something Tony was not able to do, so I guess I was yearning for attention and time. Later that morning, around 8:00 a.m., I got a knock on the door. It was Tony and when I answered the door he immediately knew that Richard was in my house because he knew what kind of car Richard drove. When I first opened the door, I was terrified, because I did not know how Tony was going to react, plus Richard was a police officer at that time.

Fortunately, they did not fight, but they did get in each other's face. Richard was about three times the size of Tony. So, when Tony got into his face, Richard said, "Look man if I put my hands on you, you will probably break apart!" "So, please get out of my face!"

When Richard made that statement, I immediately begged Tony to just leave and not to cause any trouble. I asked Richard to stop arguing with Tony. I was torn between two lovers, feeling like a fool!

Tony was such a gentleman and I did not want anybody to get hurt on account of my bad judgment. I really did care for Tony.

Well, after the confrontation at my apartment, I just wanted to have some alone time and I asked Richard to leave as well. A few weeks went by and I did not hear from either of them. Then Tony called me and wanted to talk to me. That was reassuring to know that he still cared. On the other hand, Richard disappeared and did not call me back right away.

This man was once my sugar daddy and I got kind of spoiled. He brought me a car, paid my utilities, and always paid whenever we would go out, but he was also notorious for twisting the truth.

In fact, the next week I went out with one of my girlfriends and I spotted Richard in the Sheraton Hotel sitting on a sofa rapping with a woman. My girlfriend and I had planned to visit the club inside the hotel. At first, I thought the woman was just someone he was just having a casual conversation with. Maybe he had to moonlight at the club? Matter of fact, the last time I spoke to him was the evening before. He said that he had to make a run to New York with a friend of his. Well, I guess his run was with the lady I found him with that night. I never said anything to him and just proceeded to the club with my girlfriend

Karen. She could tell that I was very annoyed and embarrassed about the situation.

Actually, I felt embarrassed and uneasy because I just knew in my heart that this man only wanted me, so I thought. Especially, since he spent a lot of time with me. It was truly a wake up call for me. After that incident, no more than a month later, he married that woman.

So, questions started popping up in my head; "How long did he know her and why did he get married so soon? Life goes on and sometimes the roller coaster ride can take you in different directions, dips, jerks and sudden stops.

Where do I go from here? I was disgusted with myself and alone. So, I picked up the phone and called Tony and asked him if he wanted to come over. Remember, I dropped him for Richard, so I guess I was just getting back what I dished out! Tony and I were not able to get that spark back completely. So I just stayed single for a little while until I started working in downtown, Baltimore.

I found a new job working for Haribo of America, the company that makes gummy bears! There was no parking available, so I had to find off street parking, which was very expensive. Anyway, I starting parking at the Arrow's Parking Garage, which was two blocks from my job and very convenient.

After working at my new job for about a month, I started to notice this nice looking young man who worked as the Parking Garage Manager. Here I go again, not finishing one chapter before I go to the next one. However, he had a beautiful smile and demeanor, so I could not resist. I often talked about him to my co-worker Rochelle. Sometimes I would give Rochelle a ride home from work since she did not have any transportation. She did have a nice boyfriend who would sometimes pick her up from work. But one particular day, Rochelle's boyfriend could not pick her up from work so she asked me for a ride home. Then she asked me about the Parking Garage Manager! I told her that I want to say something to him so badly, but that I was scared!

Well, she gave me the courage to say something after he got one of the guys to bring my car to me. He was in the office talking to his co-workers and that's when I waved for him to come over. When he got to my car I said, "Did you know that you have such a beautiful smile?" After that statement, he smiled from ear to ear and then I proceeded out of the garage, giggling like a little girl. I don't know why I acted so shy?

The very next day when I arrived at the garage he was there and we spoke briefly. When I arrived at my office, I could still see his smile. So, I daydreamed all day long until I got off. As I walked towards the garage, I noticed that he had my car ready for me. However, he accidentally locked the keys in the car! He tried for a least a good hour to get the door opened, but was not successful. Then suddenly, a guy just strolling thru the garage asked us if we needed any help. The guy came over to my car and opened it in two minutes. I could tell that the Parking Garage Manager was embarrassed.

So, to make him feel special, I thanked him for trying to get the door unlocked and I told him that he could take me out to dinner. Talk about being forward!

He immediately accepted and we started dating a few days later. We hit it off right away. It was probably around the summer time when we started dating and by September we were inseparable. We played hooky from work a couple of times and drove to Washington, DC for the day. Then we would go to different places to grab a bite to eat.

He was so attentive, but shy. One day he drove my car from the parking lot to my job. Of course it was only two blocks away, but he sure had a lot of nerve, especially since I did not give him permission to drive my car. Well, I'm glad I waited because he had my car detailed and when I got in the car he gave me a kiss. Also, in the back seat were two dozen of red roses. That's why I love to receive flowers. They are very sentimental to some woman, especially to me!

MARRIED & BABY ON THE WAY

We fell in love fast! I will never forget the day he proposed to me. He asked me to marry him after five or six months of dating. I got pregnant, but later on I had a miscarriage. It was very upsetting to both of us. The miscarriage happened sometime in February, but we already had set a date to get married on 3/21/1987, which was also my Grandfather Ross's birthday. He was excited and so was I. So we invited all our friends including his family from South Carolina to our wedding.

It was a beautiful wedding. My daughter Nicole was our flower girl and my little cousin Brandon was the ring bearer. My father walked me down the aisle and my sister Dawn sung "We've Only Just Began." My husband and I cried with joy and also with fear! Not knowing what to expect, marriage can be very scary.

My cherished photo of my father and me.
My father walked me down the Aisle,
March 21, 1987

My first love Ronnie showed up at the ceremony. I did not see him, but his mother told me that he was there, but he left immediately after my husband and I exchanged vows.

Our reception was held at a school hall right across the street from my Aunt Martha's house. Again, we were young and had no money and we didn't even go on a honeymoon.

Instead, we just went somewhere locally the next day and my mother kept Nicole for me for a few days. I was glad to finally settle down and get married. I really enjoyed my new married life.

As a matter fact, one month after we were married, I got pregnant. I guess I am a fertile Girdle! Happy to be a new mom again! I thought I looked good pregnant and my husband always complimented me on how well I looked and he was very attentive to me.

He did not pressure me too much then, and did a marvelous job at the time being the head of the household. Finally, Nicole has a real father in her life. Someone who really cares for her! Life was going pretty well. My pregnancy was going find and I even started talking to my older relatives about me having another baby in a few years. Of Course they all looked at me like I was crazy! I assumed it was because I had not experienced anything yet, so only time would tell.

There was one obstacle that stood in the way! My husband's job had not offered their employees health insurance benefits and I was working temp work at the time of my pregnancy.

So, I did what I could do best and that was going out to find a better job for myself and my family. 4 ½ months into my pregnancy, I got a job working for a sunroom company. I was good with math and knew accounts receivable and accounts payable. So, the employment agency that I worked for called me one day to fill a 3 month assignment.

I was not showing at the time and I did not feel like I was putting myself or my child in any kind of danger, by accepting the position.

One afternoon, my supervisor at the sunroom company, called me in his office. At first I was a little apprehensive and was not sure why he wanted to see me. He started off by saying how pleased he was with my work and then he offered the position to me permanently. I got a pay increase and would be eligible for insurance after 60 days.

Well, exactly sixty days later, on October 9, 1987, I went into labor early. I was not due to have my child until December 1987. That day I felt a little nauseous and did a lot of walking. I had left work early, because I had to go to the courthouse to pay for a fine that we got for a parking ticket. A flag was placed on our vehicle registration and our tags were scheduled to expire that day!

Then, that evening I called my doctor and told him about my symptoms and he told me that if my symptoms got worse to go to the hospital. Well, that night I received an unexpected visit from my cousin George. He had stopped by to see my husband, but I told him that he was at work and would not get home until 7-7:30pm that evening. Well. I am glad George stayed, because I started having sharp pains in my stomach. I was not supposed to have the baby until December!

I asked George to take me to the hospital and I called my husband and told him to meet me at the hospital because I thought I was in labor! Of course he was nervous, and could not remember how to get there. Meanwhile, I proceeded to the hospital and after I arrived, approximately half hour later my husband came. By the time he got there, I was being examined and the nurse sad that I had a fever and that I had started to dilate. Apparently, the amniotic fluid that protects the baby had come out and I did not know it. Trying to put two and two together, I did remember falling on the last step of my mother house about two weeks prior. But I felt find and the baby did not show any signs of distress, so I assumed all was well. All was not well, because the fluid had seeped out slowly over the two week period and caused me to go into labor, which ultimately caused me to have my daughter.

At approximately 11:30 pm Kelly was born into the world, only weighing 2lbs 15 ounces.

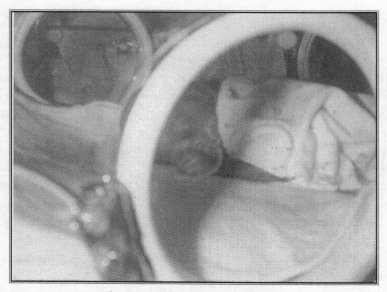

**Photo #1 of Kelly in the NICU
(Neonatal Intensive Care Unit)**

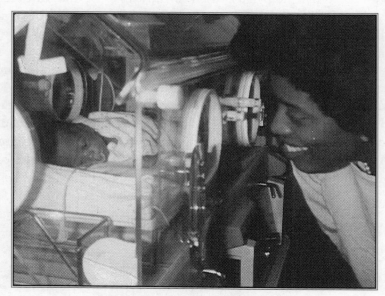

**Photo #2 of Kelly in the NICU
(Neonatal Intensive Care Unit)**

Immediately after she was born, she was placed in an incubator and I could not hold her right away. Neither was I able to take her home when it was time for me to be discharge from the hospital. She was placed in the neonatal intensive care unit. I became very distraught and scared because I never seen a baby that small in my life. Plus when the doctor talked to my husband and me, he told us that there could be complications because of our daughter's low birth weight and also she could possibly have learning disabilities. I was not as concerned about the learning disabilities as I was with her overall health.

She was given oxygen because she had Respiratory Distress Syndrome, and we also had to make sure she did not have excessive bleeding of her brain. All those challenges are what my husband and I had to face, which put added stress on our marriage. God is still good because the day before I went into labor is when my health insurance kicked in. She stayed in the hospital for two months because of her low birth weight. I could not bring her home until she gained at least 2 ½ more pounds. Two weeks before Christmas, I got the best Christmas gift ever! Little Kelly was able to come home and be with her family. Previously, I had to go to the hospital everyday to see her and it was very painful not be able to bring my baby home. I was truly drained mentally and emotionally.

The first two years of our marriage was bliss. One day my husband ran into a couple of his friends from South Carolina on the Metro Station. We lived right near the subway station so commuting was easy for us. Plus, we only had one car at that time. The friends he ran into were is former classmates, Barbara and Don. Ironically, they got married on 3/21/1987 as well! They had a few kids, so we often got together with them at our house or theirs'. All our kids got along well and everything was fine, except the fact that my husband behavior started changing.

Now, he always went to work and that was not the problem, but I discovered that he became a different person.

He reminded me of my Grandfather Ross. He would come home drunk from work quite often and my grandmother would argue with him every time he got home. I felt like I was living in her shoes. I had a man who paid the bills, but became a different person when he drank too much.

So my advice to anyone reading this novel is to research the individual and make sure you meet his /her family before you say I do.

ABUSED & WOUNDED

The man I married became the night of the living dead! He totally started changing his demeanor and his attitude towards his family. Unfortunately, our relationship started drifting apart. We began to argue with each other as if it was a way of life for us. First of all, we both were not ready to get married or even have children.

For men, just because you have a penis does not mean you're ready for responsibility or that you will make a great father. It has to be something that you are committed to do. And for woman, having reproductive capabilities does not necessarily mean that you're ready for womanhood or motherhood either. It takes sacrifice and commitment from the man and the woman. Also, it takes a special person to admit when they are not ready for marriage and at least be willing to put a stop to something that could inevitably have a disastrous outcome. Well, being closed minded, stubborn and a miss no it all, caused me to encounter several more **cycles of pain** before I starting realizing the causes and effects.

I believe that I rushed into getting married, because I was the last one left at home and my mother started getting on my case about every little thing. So, I became anxious about leaving home. Now of course in hindsight, I know that my mother was just trying to steer me in the right direction.

I don't blame my spouse for everything that happened to us. However, I know if we were taught and prepared to become responsible adults and parents we may have been able to avoid some of the marital struggles/pitfalls that occurred. Now, as my spouse and I continue to live this dysfunctional life, the relationship only got worse.

We began to resent and dislike each other so badly, that we forgot our children would most likely suffer the consequences of our actions. There were several situations our children were exposed to. For example, fighting was the biggest obstacle and then emotional turmoil was the next culprit. The fighting between my spouse and I got so ugly, and believe me I'm so ashamed of our actions toward each other.

Also, I forgot to mention that a year later after I had Kelly, I was blessed to work for one of the largest home builders in Maryland (Winchester Homes). They trained me well and I knew all the phases of how a house is built.

This position enabled me to understand project management, and how to communicate well with supervisors in the field. I really loved that job and was happy with my position. Unfortunately, I worked in pain almost daily during my entire stay there and my employer never knew it. My spouse was not happy with his employer and became somewhat jealous of me and the position that I had. I did my best to be in his corner by helping him find another position.

So, I helped him prepare his resume, since that was something that I was good at doing. He did get a job working at the hotel in the concierge department. His self esteemed got a little better, but his thirst for alcohol increased. He started using drugs and showed signs of addiction when he became more verbally abusive towards me, as well as irresponsible when it came to picking up our daughter Kelly from day care on time. I would always have to apologize to the day care center for my husband's tardiness.

Not to mention I had just faced another **cycle of pain**, when my grandmother was rushed to the hospital. She was never sick and one day when she was coming back from her trip to North Carolina, she got sick on the train and the very next day she was admitted to Good Samaritan Hospital, for having suffered a heart attack. Because I had to wait for my husband to come from work, I did not get a chance to go to the hospital until her second or third day there. Let's just say I was battling with some issues at home that I deeply regretted later. I spoke to my grandmother the second day that she was there and asked her how she was feeling, she replied, "I'm doing just fine, don't worry about me baby."

Of course I did worry and I said, "I will be by to see you tomorrow (day three)." Well, after hearing her voice I felt relieved and comforted, until the very next day, when my mother received a call from the hospital, we were told that she had taken a turn for the worse and that the family needed to come quickly. "How could this be?" I said to my mother, "I just spoke to her last night and she was doing fine." My mother and the rest of my grandmother's family rushed to the hospital as soon as we got the call. When the family arrived we were asked to stay in the family room for a little while, until further notice. We all were pacing the hospital waiting room. Suddenly, a doctor came out to talk to us and he told us that, "He was sorry to tell us the bad news, but your love one has passed." All of the family members gasped for air and cried profusely. My cousin Johnny ran down the hall crying and grabbing his head, my mother and her sibling cuddled together and cried profusely. Later we asked the staff if we could see her before they take her to the morgue. Only a few family members were able to see her at a time. So, I was able to go with the first group and when I approached her bedside, it was as if she was sleeping and the blood in her body was still warm. I just stared and grabbed her hands and kissed them and asked her to forgive me for not being present to see her while she still had breath in her body. We all stayed in the roomed until her body became cold. It was an overwhelming situation to be put in.

A week later, we had her funeral at her church, "Southern Baptist". It was packed and every seat was filled to full capacity. When I approached the casket, I thought I was looking at an angel, she was dressed in a white dress and she looked 30 years younger. She was beautiful and had a peaceful look on her face.

Losing my grandmother, the pillar of our family was so hard on everyone. It was very hard for me to hold it together during my grieving period. However, I will say that knowing the Lord helped me overcome the pain and sadness of losing my grandmother. I will never forget her and while I was writing this section about her death, I cried again, because of the great memories that I had with her.

My relationship with my husband did not get better. If I had to do it all over again, I would have left much sooner. No one should subject themselves to misery and distress especially under those circumstances.

A year and a half later I got a job working as a rental processing clerk. The job was pretty stressful, but I was determined to learn how to process new leases, move- ins & move outs applications. Everyday when I went to work, my heart was heavy from my failing marriage. Again, no one on the job knew what I was feeling inside. And to make matters worse, I worked with this girl from hell, she was racist and did not want to show me how to process the paperwork for my position.

This was added stress that I had to battle each day. It was difficult for me to be a wife and a mother. Sometimes, I thought I was having a mental breakdown.

For two months, while I was at work I would go in the ladies room to cry my heart out, just to release my inner pain and anxiety.

I prayed everyday to God and asked him to please provide me with some kind of refuge and protection. Well, my prayers were answered. You see God may not come when you want him to, but he is always on time. God made a way of escape for me. He knew how much I could handle and He would not let me fall. The next day after I had a talk with God, I over heard one of the property managers with my company say that they lost one of the rental managers for one of their properties. They needed someone immediately and did not know what to do. Well, one thing about me, I am very assertive and not afraid to ask questions.

So, I interjected and excused myself and asked the property manager to consider me for the position. I told her that I was very good with people, that I was a quick learner and that I think I would be a perfect candidate for the job.

Besides, I had already gained some experience with doing the processing of the rents, move-ins and move-outs paperwork. Well, the manager was very impressed with my assertiveness and reasoning. So, she told me that she would give it some thought and get back with me. Well, the next day I got the news that I needed to hear.

The rental manager job was offered to me and I started the next week. No more frustrations at work with my co-worker, thank you JESUS! I became stronger and more determined. This allowed me to take a good look at myself and my purpose in life and the abilities that I had to offer.

Now, I still had my problems at home, but they became more tolerable because I had some happiness to keep me going. I received a promotion at work, I worked directly with the public and I got a chance to communicate. So, when I went home, I was able to block out the negative energy that was trying to enter into my space.

I had a real good friend who I could confide in and every time I would mention to this friend that I was leaving my spouse, he would just nod and shake his head. From time to time, he would put his two cents in and tell me that I needed to live a better life for my kids and myself. I just would tell him how much I loved my husband and that he was once a fantastic man. Of course that's before he got addicted to drugs. Once again, I was in relationship denial and became very co-dependent.

I refused to believe that I was living a dysfunctional life and how it was destroying me and my girls. It was not fair. I wanted my girls to have a father in their lives. I did not want them to live without a dad, like myself. Not having my father in my life was very painful and I did not want my girls to experience the same **cycle of pain** that I had gone through. So, I thought that I was doing them a favor, by staying with a man who had issues that nearly destroyed us: mentally, physically and emotionally.

Well, one morning when I went to work, I started imagining what life would be like without the stress. So, I began to contemplate separating from my spouse. It was time and I no longer had the strength to endure my spouse's negative behavior any longer.

So, I called my buddy, my sister, and a few relatives to help me move. I had made this decision to leave my spouse rather quickly because I got tired.

I found a new apartment and put down a security deposit. I planned the move two weeks after I made up my mind. Meanwhile, I continued to go home each night and deal with the monster that my husband had become. I knew it was not him, but the evil spirit that had taken residence over his body.

THE COURAGE TO LEAVE

I'll never forget the evening when my husband came home intoxicated as usual and wanted to pick a fight with me because I was on the phone and he wanted me to come to bed to have sex. Well, I was used to the routine and I did not want him to suspect that I was planning to leave the next morning. So, I went along with the routine, because I knew that I was about to become a free woman in the next 10 hours. Free from pain and free to be who I wanted to be. I was talking to his best friend's wife, Barbara and she knew what my plans were, and just told me to contact her whenever I could.

Well, the next morning my husband gave me a kiss before he went to work. This was his routine! So, when he kissed me, I kissed him back. Now, after he left for work I got up and I called my family members and friends that everything was a go. My spouse was gone to work and now I can move out. I moved out of the apartment in 4 hours and into my new place.

The very next day when I was on my way to work, I turned into the apartment community where I worked and right as I turned in, my husband was standing on the corner crying and waiting for me. I did not now what to expect, because I left and took everything from our apartment and when he came home, I'm sure it was devastating for him to lose his family and to come home to an empty house. Well, it was a wake up call for him for a little while.

I hated to leave my spouse, but life with him was so miserable at that time and we never went to counseling!

We only talked about what happened and why it happened. The same male friend told me not to give in too soon and to let my spouse realize the mistakes he made. He even told me about the time he lost his family because of his past drinking problems. He said to me that letting him back in my life too soon would caused him to repeat his past behavior and he also said that my spouse needed to learn to appreciate his family and what he has lost.

I did not listen to my friend and less than three weeks, I allowed my husband back in. So, the **cycle of pain** started all over again. Again, I was yearning for love and thought I needed his presence to make me complete. I felt very empty without him and wanted my marriage to work. I came from a broken home and I did not want to repeat the cycle. I realized that I was holding on to what I lost when my parents separated. Sometimes it's necessary to let go, especially if you're doing a disservice to yourself and your family.

Well, the cycle continued because my spouse was very nice for the first 3 months, but afterwards he started his same behavior again. Remember a leopard doesn't change it spots! My good friend tried to warn me earlier, but I would not listen. I was in a relationship denial. Actually, it was as if I had a thorn in my side and I did not know how to remove it. A thorn is painful, but you can become numb to it just like anything else you allow to control you. These controlling mechanisms are strongholds.

Like I said earlier, my husband's behavior was intolerable. Yet, I still stayed with him. Then I started really resenting him and my behavior towards men started to change. I remember there were times when I treated him like a child in order to make sure he brought his money home.

He got paid every Friday and every Friday I had to be at his job to pick up his check. I had to do this to make sure the bills would get paid and to keep my spouse in check. Yes, I became very controlling. Not by choice, but I had no other options at that time. As I mentioned earlier in the book, this was something that God has told me to reveal to others in order to help bring a change in how we treat each other. Hopefully this book will provide some guidance to those who have experienced similar types of pain. Remember these three points; people are generally in a storm, going through a storm or coming out of a storm. Storms do not last forever and will eventually clear up after awhile. You just have to learn how to ride them out and wait for them to clear up.

However, the storm that I was in with my spouse seemed like eternity. Still no change! I truly thought in my mind that I could get him to change back to that loving man I married. Unfortunately, he got worse before he got better.

HOPING FOR A CHANGE

My poor babies, Nicole and Kelly had to see their father's uncontrollable behavior. We continued to fight and argue everyday. Here we go again, I moved to another new place a year later, hoping that the move would bring about a positive change.

The new place was the third floor apartment above my mother's. I knew for sure that my spouse would get his act together because we moved just above my mother. Plus, I felt safe being close to home. We lived in a duplex apartment that had five units in it and my mother lived on the first floor. Meanwhile, while I was on the phone with my sister, my husband was yelling and shouting horrible things about my family. Then he snatched the phone out of my hand and pulled the phone out of the socket. Do you know that approximately 15 minutes later, the door bell rang?

It was my sister, she lived on the east side of Baltimore and she managed to get to our place in fifteen minutes, which actually should have taken 30 minutes. I guess she was so furious with my husband and she came prepared to whip his butt. My husband shouted! "Who is it?" She replied, "It's me and open up this damn door." I buzzed her in and my husband immediately said to my sister, "Tammy, my beef is not with you (sound like Doc Holiday in Tombstone) and she said, "Oh yes it is, whenever you threaten or talk about anybody in my family, it's on!" I had to hold my laugh in. I felt like I had just gotten rescued by superwoman!

Two months later, I put my husband out and my sister and her husband moved in with me. They were in the process of buying a house and suggested that they would stay with me to help me out. They paid towards the rent and helped me out with the kids. My husband moved in with his cousin, who lived not too far from my apartment. He begged me to let him come back home. Whenever I would take him back, he was only good for three months.

I admit that I was a very weak woman at that time and was just trying to hold onto to what I thought was normal.

I started to visit him at his cousin's place and of course we started to hug and make love and those feeling started to come back. Then a month later, I had a talk with my sister and her husband and asked them if they would not mind staying with my mother, who lived on the first floor because my husband and I were getting back together. They both looked at me as if I had three heads and said, "I think it's a bad idea, but we can't tell you what to do with your marriage." They still joke with me today about me putting them out when they came to rescue me.

Well, a hard head makes a soft derriere! Months after my sister and her husband moved in their house, I called them to see if I could live with them this time, because that evil spirit that has been living inside my spouse came back with vengeance. He did not want to leave this time, so I left! I left all my furniture and my clothes. Just like Jamie Foxx used to say, "I am ret to go!" When my spouse found out I was leaving him, he threw me on the floor like a wrestler in front of our daughter Kelly. She was 5 years old at that time and the next morning when I took her to school, the first thing she said to me when we arrived to her school was, "Mommy, why did daddy throw you down on the floor like that?" I was so embarrassed and shame had taken residence in my spirit.

I made up something so that she would not discuss it with her teacher. Then a few days later, she became angry with me because I would not allow her father to visit me or her. She did not understand what was happening at that time.

Well, one thing about me, I am a go getter and I knew that I had to find an apartment, so that I could bring my family together (Nicole, Kelly and me). Nicole stayed with my other sister Dawn temporarily. I found a two bedroom apartment in Owings Mills, Maryland. I selected that apartment, because I wanted to be as far away as possible from my husband. But for some reason, I felt so dependant on him. I was doing it all along myself, but I could not **break the cycle** then. I stayed in contact with him from a distance, but months later he wooed himself back into my life. Begging for forgiveness and telling me that he's changed. He even started going to church and gave his life to God. So, I thought!

My husband had gotten two great jobs that allowed me to stay home! Something, I always wanted to be able to do! My mother always worked two or three jobs while I was little and I truly desired to have her home with me!

So, staying home had empowered me and gave me a chance to exhale. My brain and my heart finally stopped racing and I felt some normalcy in my life finally. Until, my husband had a setback. It's amazing, I knew my husband like the back of my hand. I could tell whenever he was getting ready to have a setback or whenever he would start his drinking binge. Sure enough that's what exactly happened! My husband started showing signs of drug abuse again. He started snapping at me and the kids. Then, he stopped showing up for his job with UPS. One evening, I got a call from one of the manager's at UPS. It was a lady and she was very polite. She said, "I'm very concerned about your husband because it is not like him not to show up for work." "He is very good at his job." She asked me if I knew where he was. I made up some excuse, but felt like I had to tell her that he was having some personal problems. She was willing to save his job for him, but she needed to hear from him soon. Of course, he never contacted the lady and he lost that job. I was so disgusted with him because he lost a job that provided our entire family with health and dental coverage, something we needed badly.

Also, keep in mind, I did not see my husband for seven whole days and several things ran across my mind. First of all, I knew that I had to move and get out of this dysfunctional relationship and I did not want my choices to affect my kids. I loved my apartment, but I had no peace there, so I had to move again! I just needed the strength to do it!

MINI BREAKDOWN

April of 1994 was supposed to be the turning point for my life. I finally left my husband for good. The week before I moved, I was home alone sitting in my favorite comfortable chair. Rocking back and forth and having severe migraine headaches. I cried out to God and asked him to help me get through my pain. I even called on a nurse because I felt like I possibly had a brain aneurysm. I could not breathe and I felt like I had to faint. She advised me to go to the hospital just to make sure it wasn't anything too serious. Well, after I got off the phone with the nurse, I immediately turned my attention to the God and His word. I literally crawled in to my bedroom and picked up the Bible off my nightstand. The first book of the Bible that I turned to was Psalms 37 (I had never read this book prior to this incident). I began to read all the verses associated with this book. One verse in particular stood out the most, "Do Not Fret", is what the first verse said. It was as if God was in the room with me looking at me and telling me not to worry. Before I grabbed the Bible, I forgot to tell you that I felt like someone had stabbed me in my stomach and once I read all verses, the pain went away and I felt like a new person.

I was able to get myself together mentally and emotionally. So, I called my sister and asked her if I could stay with her while going through my transition. She talked to her husband and they both agreed to let me stay on the second floor of their house. The duplex house had a separate entrance, which they had planned to rent out. But instead, they allowed me and my girls to live there for only $200 per month. However, even back then it was hard for me to pay the $200. My God when will life get easier for me!

I was not making that much money at the time and was not prepared to handle the expenses for the rent. So, I knew I had to make some changes that would allow me to be in a better position to care for my family. I refused to contact my spouse since I felt as though he **abandoned** his responsibilities by moving to South Carolina to stay with his mother. Here I go again; I was put in the position to be a single parent again. Sick and tired of being sick and tired.

I needed a way out of this cage of confusion and bondage. I was in pain and feelings of despair began to take a toll on me. I became very depressed and distraught. I felt like a failure and did not have the self-esteem to get my self together back then.

To make matters worse, I ran into the man that molested me when I was 15 years old. The wound was re-opened and there was nothing I could do to stop my heart and soul from bleeding. The pain felt like someone had poured alcohol in a huge open wound. It was very excruciating and too much for me to bare.

Remember, nobody knew that I had been molested. So, the secret began to haunt me and follow me like a dark shadow or cloud. The way that I ran into him again was crazy and bizarre. When people say that we live in a small world there is definitely some truth to that. Out of all the people in the world, my sister befriended this woman who lived next to her, who happen to be one of the molester's sister. You see, his sister was not the problem; it was her brother, the guy that molested me.

Just think, this was 18 years later, and I still felt like I had been molested again. I was on my way to my upstairs apartment when I heard a faint voice call my name....Leslie, Leslie, Leslie! I thought that I was dreaming because I recognized that voice but did not want to look-up and see who was calling me. I took one quick glance and I almost passed out before I got into my apartment. I had groceries in my hand and my kids by my side. My kids knew something was wrong with me because I immediately shutdown. I dropped the groceries, closed myself in my bedroom and asked my oldest daughter to take over with putting the items up and feeding her little sister. I thank God my daughter was mature for her age. She was such a big help to me much more than she'll ever realize.

Keep in mind, my children and my family did not have a clue to what was going on with me. They all assumed the reason why I isolated myself was because of my marital separation, although, that did contribute to my depression. I did experience a flashback at that time. I could see myself being molested all over again and I could see him thrashing his penis into me over and over again, I could see the fetus falling in the pan over an over again. I could see the interns asking the doctor what was happening and what type of procedure I was getting over and over again. I wanted to scream so badly, but nothing would come out and I literally froze, with my body in a catatonic state.

Well, later that evening, I experience some very sharp pains in my stomach and did not have an appetite for anything. So, I decided to take myself to the emergency room to seek help for my sickness. I just wanted my family to believe that it was related to being exhausted and emotionally tired, not my molestation experience. Since, I was still ashamed and embarrassed to even talk about it to anyone; I was not ready to talk to anybody, except God!

I remember when I got to the emergency room the doctor asked me if I was under some kind stress? I replied to him and said, "I just separated from my spouse and that's what probably contributed to my illness." He agreed and suggested that I go and seek counseling and perhaps there would be someone that could help me get through this pain.

I followed his instructions and found a woman counselor. She was not quite as warm as I expected and I decided to end my sessions with her. She did convince me to talk to my family and to get everything off my chest. So after my last session with her, I decided to call for a family meeting. The meeting included my sisters and my mother. I began the meeting with prayer, because I needed God to guide me through this secret that I held for over 18 years. As the words came out, I began to feel brave and of course I wept as I revealed my molestation secret to my family. My kids were not included in the meeting because I felt as though they were too young to fully understand what I was going through. However, they knew that I was going through something.

The family meeting was very touching, because I got a positive reaction from my family. Initially, I thought that they would judge me and scrutinize my actions. Instead, they consoled me, hugged me and said that they wished I had revealed the molestation secret to them sooner.

The way that I mentioned it in the beginning of this book is the way that I described it to them. My mother and sisters cried and were stunned and upset about my ordeal. They gave me the best support at that time to help me get through this **cycle of pain**.

My mother's heart was heavy and my sisters were angry with the man that molested me. Now, that my sister found out the truth about my pain, it was hard for her to even look into her neighbor's eyes, without seeing her neighbor's brother (the molester). I had asked my sister not to say anything to her neighbor about the incident between her brother and me. I told her that God would take care of everything. Also, I wanted to close that chapter to the book in my life, but that has been a difficult task for me to do. You can forgive, but you will never forget a traumatic experience.

RECOVERY PERIOD

Oh, how good that felt to finally let somebody know how painful my life had been for 18 years. You see, silence is not golden all the time, especially whenever you encounter a life changing event that could either make you or break you. Fortunately, I was able to recover and my world started to feel at peace, at least for a short while.

As time went on, I asked my mother if she could help me get a car so that I would not be limited to the type and location of job that I needed to support my family. She trusted me and decided to co-sign for a vehicle even before I got a better job that would allow me to make the car payments. Tell me that was not God! She truly helped me get back on my feet. I Love Her So Much For That! Also, I thank God for giving me a mother that has always been in my corner and never stop believing in me.

Well, life appeared to be looking up for me. After I revealed my pain to my sisters and mother, the blessing started coming out the wood work. I got a new car, new job, moved in a rental townhouse and I met a new man. I was on my way of having my soul healed and revitalized. Again, I thought that I was ready to move forward. I had met someone who was crazy about me and my kids and he was always in my company. This left me little time to think about any existing pain. What else do I need? I've found love and now I can move on.

Well, that's not true. You see, moving on was okay but moving on before you're ready is not okay. I continued to repress the abandonment pain I felt from my first husband. And, I still had not healed totally from my molestation experience. Not only did that man violate my body, he placed a dark cloud over my head for years to follow. I did not close the book to the chapter before opening another book. Don't you know that it's very important to examine your feelings and resolve any unsolved issues you have with others and especially yourself, before proceeding to another relationship?

I wish I had found a book like this to at least give me some guidance, some directions and answers to my problems. Not just any words, but words and advice that can pertain to your life. This can be very powerful when it comes to revitalizing your broken spirit and soul. So, I guess that's why I am so passionate to help others who have experienced **cycles of pain** in their lives.

My focus was improving and I had decided to make some life changing decisions, like buy a home. When I mentioned this to my immediate family, they kind of chuckled. I guess in their eyes, it was impossible for a single woman with kids to buy a house, with a fair credit rating. Remember, my mother never owned a house and my sisters owned their houses with their spouse. So, here little old broke me deciding to take a chance to become a home owner.

I have always been the type of person to write down my goals. That way I would know if I am on track to fulfill them. I had an excellent rental history, so I figured if I got approved for a mortgage it would be based on common sense lending. My job history was not consistent at the time and frankly I never saw myself working for any company for a lifetime. I always wanted to explore and become more marketable. So, I started this quest to find a house for my girls and me. My best friend Gail has always been a supporter and told me to go for it and so I did. I contacted a Realtor from O'Conor Piper & Flynn at that time. The Realtor was a man and he was very obliging. He never questioned my ability to buy, but simply gave me the tools and advice I needed to buy a house.

I will never forget when he asked me, "How much money do you have towards settlement?" I told him that I had zero dollars and that the money is coming." He simply said, "Okay!" So, I began to strategize and asked my sister and mother if they would help me with the closing cost. Fortunately, my settlement date was scheduled three months after I placed a contract on the house. The sellers were purchasing a Condo that was not going to be ready to move-in until August 1997. So, this gave me more time to get my settlement money together. A month before closing, my sister said that she could loan me $2,500 towards closing and then the very next day, my mother stop past my place and said that she just got a credit card in the mail with $10,000 credit limit. She agreed to loan me $2,000. **"Faith is the substance of things hope for and the evidence of things not seen."**

God has always been on time. You know the old saying, "He may not come when you want him to come, but he is always on time when you need him."

That statement definitely applied to me because everything started to fall into place when I needed the funds to complete my big purchase.

Meanwhile, I had to still explain to the underwriting department why I encountered some credit issues in the past. I had to sell them on my creditworthiness as well. I did exactly what underwriting asked for. I put together a letter listing in chronological order the reasons for the negative marks on my credit report and why I felt that I should receive the mortgage for my home purchase.

It was the most stressful time in my life, especially towards the end of the loan process. I was taking care of my father, raising my girls, attending school part time and working a fulltime job. I wanted to scream on several occasions, but I kept my eyes on the prize, and continued my quest to get the house. I will never forget the day before closing. I had not yet received an okay from the mortgage company that I was approved for the loan. I started to give up, but the loan processor told me to just reply to whatever the underwriting department wanted. Back then I did not have a cell phone, just a pager. The last paged I got was from the loan processor. She left me a message on my phone telling me to call her because she had something important to tell me.

She did not sound enthusiastic, but very stern and direct. So, I assume that the news would probably be unfavorable. When I called her back, her first words were, "Did you get my message?" I replied "Yes," and asked her what is the status of my loan? She said, "Leslie, I have some news for you!" I said, "What news?" She said, "You got the house!" I cried with excitement and thanked her for all her help. Afterwards, I called my mother and Mr. Carr the man my mother had been dating all those years answered the phone. He said, "What's the matter?" I explained to him that I was crying because I was happy and that I got the house. So, he immediately put my mother on the phone and told her that I was crying for a good reason and not to be alarmed!

On August 29, 1997, the day of settlement was a dream come true and I had to pinch myself. My settlement went well and I moved in a few days later. I loved being a home owner and immediately started decorating my home. Decorating has always been something that I enjoyed doing. The girls were glad to move in a house and they adjusted very well. Also, my father moved in with us and seemed comfortable and happy to be there.

My relationship with my new friend continued, but my heart was still heavy and torn. I was not sure if I was even ready for the relationship that I was in. I enjoyed my company with my new friend, but there was a seven-year difference between us.

Well, after dating my new friend for a few years, I started feeling anxiety from the relationship and we decided to take a break from the relationship for a little while. Remember, I had not allowed myself any time to heal and I still was not sure of what I needed at that time.

AS THE CYCLE TURNS

I continued to date and after, the 5th year of separation from my spouse, I felt I was ready to divorce and move on with my life. I tried to skip the part where you go through stages of anger, grief, pain and forgiveness. Because, I did not want to feel any pain, so I avoided it as much as possible. The marriage between my spouse and I dissolved, and I remember on the final day of our divorce, I went over to my girlfriends house and starting break dancing. This was done to celebrate a new beginning for me. Initially my heart was heavy, and I thought that after everything was finalized, it would be the end of my pain. Well, that was not the case, because, we left a scar that had never healed and it was passed down to our children and other relationships to come.

After I divorced my spouse in February 1999, a few months later, my father died. Then six months later, in September/October of 1999 my mother almost died from a blood clot that traveled to her lung. It was God's grace that kept her.

Meanwhile, let me tell you about my father's last days on this earth! I took my father's death a lot harder than I anticipated. Although he was not in my life when I was younger, I grew closer to him in 1994, that's when he was first diagnosed with lung cancer. He stayed at an apartment building not far from my sister and me. And unfortunately, my father did not do so well there. He also started to develop dementia real bad. So, after he moved from the apartment, I agreed to have him stay with me and the girls. It was nice having their grandfather there, since they both had not had that experience before. Now, watching my father had its' trials. My father not only had problems with his lung, but he also had dementia. He would often leave the house with the door wide opened. By the time my girls got home from school, they were scared to go inside. I had to leave work or call my sister and ask her to check things out.

Oh! I'll never forget the time my father wanted to go to the store so bad that he did the unthinkable thing! I got a phone call from my youngest daughter and she said, "Mom, guess what Daddy Les tried to do?" I said, "What?" She said, "He tried to ride your bike to Wawa's so that he could get some cigarettes, but he crashed into a park car!" I immediately drove home and found a trail of blood leading down in the basement where my father slept. He was lying back on the bed as if nothing happened.

Keep in mind, my father, had also suffered a stroke years prior, and it had affected his walk. So in his condition there was no way for him to be able to ride my bike. I continued to probe him for an explanation and he said that he wanted to get out the house. I said, "Daddy you could have killed yourself!"

He just hunched his shoulders. Dear God; Please help me with my other child! He actually got worse and had to be placed in assisted living care, and a year later, his health took a turn for the worst. March of 1999, he was placed in the **Fort Hood Hospice** and my sisters and I visited him everyday. Remember when I mentioned earlier in the novel that my oldest sister Tammy really resented him. Well, she was the one who barely left his side.

My father did go to church with us frequently before he got ill and he accepted Christ in his life. So, watching him die slowly was painful, but knowing that his soul was going to be alright was the reassurance that my sisters and I had.

My father could barely grasp for air, but he did tell each of us how much he loved us and that he was sorry for not being there for us. We told him that we loved him and that we forgave him and not to worry about that right now! We video tapped my father and told him how much we love him.

Later that evening, I went home with a sense of peace in my soul and thanked God for the time I had with him. So, I decided to go back to work and keep my self busy. Plus, I was still a single parent and I needed to make some money to meet my expenses. Well, the next evening I stopped past my girlfriend Gail's house and after I was there for about 15 minutes, I got a page from my sister Dawn. I called her back and she said that Daddy was gone! I said okay and asked her, "What time did he die?" She said that when she and my other sister were arriving for a visit that is when he took his last breath, On April 2, 1999(Ironically, he died on my mother's birthday). And it seemed like he waited for my mother, before he died.

My mother had just returned from Las Vegas with her friend, Mr. Carr and she managed to see my dad a few days before he took his last breath.

So, when I got off the phone, my girlfriend Gail asked me if I was alright and I replied, "Yes, I will be fine." It did not hit me until I left her house ten minutes later. I had my youngest daughter with me and she kept asking me what was wrong with me. I told her nothing at first and then I told her that Daddy Les died tonight. I started crying out loud and then she followed. I knew that it was over and I had to release my pain. I tried to be strong and wait until I got home, but my emotions took the best of me. I miss my father to this day and wish I had an opportunity to have the father and daughter relationship that I longed for!

DADDY'S FUNERAL & MOM'S
CLOSE CALL WITH DEATH

My father had a beautiful home going service. Several friends and family members were there to show their support. Also, some of my father's former co-workers attended and made some beautiful and funny remarks about my father. His nephew, Michael read a beautiful statement that he prepared and spoke highly of my father.

My sisters and I picked out his suit and other attire for his funeral and we also put together a beautiful collage of all of us. We had pictures of my father and us when we were young girls, teenagers, and women. There were also photos of him with my children and a picture when he and my mother had happy times together. Also, his youngest sister Ernestine put together a link that showed that a link was broken. The broken link represented my father's death.

Celebration of Life

for

Leslie James Jackson

Sunrise: June 25, 1935   *Sunset: April 2, 1999*

After the funeral, we went straight to Garrison Forest Cemetery. It was a beautiful ceremony even though it was sad. We could not go near the grave site because the ground was too wet. They place a hoist around my father's casket and slowly lowered him in the ground. It was a sad day for me and when I got home, I could still smell my father's scent in the house. Some of his apparel and his travel case were at my house. So, when I had my alone moments, I would smell his clothes, cry and talk to God about my pain. My mother flew back to Las Vegas and she must have felt my pain because she mailed a card to me and enclosed was a beautiful letter. She first told me how much she loved me and then she said some reassuring words in her letter that helped me get through my depressing moments.

After a few months, my pain had subsided some and I began to feel a little better. My best friend Gail called me and asked me if I wanted to go to the Bahamas? She said that she would pay the deposit and for me to just pay the balance, when we got to the Bahamas. Well, that was the best trip that I had ever taken. I enjoyed my self tremendously. We stayed at the Marriott Hotel in Cable Beach, Bahamas.

When I arrived back home, I started feeling a little empty again, but was able to work. I worked as a Design Consultant for an upscale furniture company. At that time, my working atmosphere was very comfortable and relaxing until one horrific day.

I believe it was during the month of August when I had to open the store alone and had to work by myself for a few hours before other employees arrived. I received a phone call from one of the other stores letting me know that a customer would be by to pick up a specific table that my store had in our inventory. So, I tagged the item and made sure that it was ready for the customer once they arrived. Well, after an hour in the store this prestigious looking gentleman came in the store and asked for the table. Well, I introduced myself to him and asked him his name and if he had an order from the other store. He did have a sales receipt with him and just as I proceeded to the front counter, the phones were ringing off the hook. When I returned to the customer, I thanked him for coming in and asked him if he needed help with the table. As I extended my hand out to shake his hand, he grabbed and yanked me towards him.

Then within a few minutes, he lifted me up in the air and started grabbing and squeezing my derrière. I tried to pull myself from him, but it happened so fast and I was not expecting to be sexually assaulted.

He left abruptly once these two older ladies entered the store. I was in a complete fog and started feeling those past molestation pains again. I was violated again. I did not even help the two older ladies that came in the store. The very first person I called was my Supervisor, Nina. She told me to call the police and that she would be in as soon as possible.

Well, when the police arrived I was a mess. I could not even give a written statement, without crying. I looked up the perpetrator's information on the computer. He was a prominent doctor from Potomac Mills, Maryland. The police gave me some information to follow up with. Instead of filing charges against this guy, I just took some time off from work and later was transferred to another store, per my supervisor's request. Then after I went back to work, two months later during the month of October, I received an emergency call from Mr. Carr. My mother and Mr. Carr flew back to Las Vegas in September 1999.

Well, to receive a call from Mr. Carr is rare. So, I knew something was not right. When I first heard his voice, I felt uneasy and I knew it was something bad and I had a heavy feeling the night before!

The very first words that came out of Mr. Carr's mouth was, "Honey your mother is in ICU," and with his voice trembling. It seem like it took him 10 minutes to say those words. He said that we should try to get there as soon as possible, without any further explanation.

I immediately asked my brother in law, who is a pastor to have prayer for my mother. He and my sister Dawn were staying with me while their house was being built. So, he proceeded to have prayer and called my daughters, his wife and myself to form a prayer circle. "When two or three are joined together, God is in the mist." We each prayed to God out loud and asked him to please keep my mother. Also, during that time, I had very little money and could barely afford a plan ticket. Thank God! A good friend of the family worked for Southwest Airlines and he had (3) three buddy passes that my sisters and I could use to get to our mother. We flew out the very next day and arrived at the hospital where she was admitted. When we saw our mother for the first time, she looked like death was ready to take her out. The nurse told us that, she had a blood clot that traveled to her heart and she'll have to be placed on several different medications to save her life. My sisters and I tried to nurture our mother back to health as quick as possible. However, I was faced with a few dilemmas. My girls were still home and I needed to get back to take care of them. So, my oldest sister decided to stay with my mother. That was the hardest day for me when I kissed my mother goodbye, not knowing whether or not I would see her again. So, I prayed and asked God to put a hedge of protection around her during my absence. I felt like I was abandoning her, but I knew that God would not leave her nor forsake her.

After a few weeks in ICU, her prognosis improved and she was able to come home three weeks later. She still had to take it easy once she got back to Baltimore. She came back on Thanksgiving Day and what a Thanksgiving Day it was for my family.

My Aunt Rena, one of my mother's sisters had Thanksgiving at her house and it felt like a family reunion! It resembled the color purple scene, when (Oprah Winfrey) had just got home from being locked-up for years. Everyone was there to greet and hug my mother.

SECOND TIME AROUND

This life changing event caused me to seek out love and repress the pain again. December 1999, my boyfriend of five years proposed to me on Christmas Day and gave me an engagement ring. I thought by saying yes, I would minimize the stress, pain and the hurt that I was feeling at that time. He was very nice and attentive to me as a boyfriend, but I knew deep down inside that neither he nor I was ready for this commitment even though we had dated for five years. First of all, it was too soon, I had just divorced my daughter's father in February of 1999, my father died on April 2, 1999 and my mother almost died! And ironically, I remarried on February 14th, 2000 the same month I got divorce a year before.

Talk about trying to close a wound without cleaning it first. In addition, we eloped and nobody knew that we were getting married, except for his mother. I can remember that day as if it was yesterday.

My spouse and I tossed and turned with our decision to get marry that day (February 14, 2000). We went over to his mother's house to get ready.

He wore a nice blazer with burgundy trousers and I had purchased this beautiful royal purple 2-piece suit. The skirt had paisley print and the jacket had gold and black buttons on both sides. Just as we were leaving, his mother called him from her job and asked him to please wait. I could hear her crying through the phone.

Instead of paying attention to the signs, I refused to accept not marrying him. So, after my spouse got off the phone with his mother, he began to contemplate his decision, but he did not want to disappoint me. So, when we got ready to go to the court house, we started arguing a little bit because we were both scared. After we finished arguing we stopped by the store briefly. I was rushing him, because we had to get married before 2:30pm, since that was the latest time for the court house to perform marriages. Why was I so impatient? Now, that I look back, I know the reason why! I was tired of feeling the pain of my past and I thought by marrying him, it would solve all my problems.

Don't get me wrong, I loved him very much, but I should have allowed myself more time to heal!

As we were approaching the store, an elderly woman ran into the front of my front tire. She looked confused, we looked confused and then we stared outside the window for a few minutes.

Looking back again, it was a sign to wait. Patience is a virtue and there is a verse in the bible that says, "Be anxious for nothing."

Well, we joined hands in holy matrimony at the court house! When we arrived at the court house, there were other couples who tied the knot that day and we proudly skipped down the hall, after we said I do to each other.

However, to add insult to injury, when we arrived at our house to announce that we just got married to my kids and to my sister and her husband who were staying at my house at that time, we got blank and shock looks from everyone. My sister said to me, "Stop Lying." My brother-in-law said, "You guys are kidding, right?" Then my youngest daughter said, "Why." After hearing the negative responses from everyone, we just went upstairs like two dogs with our tails between our legs.

I locked my bedroom door and began to sob. What monster have we created? The plan was to go to the Hilton and spend the night there and to later go to Georgia for our honeymoon. By the time we arrived at the hotel, my period came on and the rest is history. All I can say was "Wow and why me, oh Lord!"

The wounds that I thought would heal had just gotten re-infected with pain, disappointment, and frustration.

After a few days past, we tried to get our girls to adjust to the new family arrangement, but it was hard needless to say.

SEPERATION CYCLE

We tried to make the best of everything. Unfortunately, the wound was not closed because my new husband and I starting having problems 6 months into the marriage and we separated in September 2000 for 1-2 months. We did not get the recommended premarital counseling that we should have gotten. What we should have done before we made the decision to marry, was to sit down and talked with my girls and get them involved with our decision. Well, that's could a, should a, what a. Also, you know the old saying I'm 21 +, +...So, I don't need anybody's advice or approval. Oh what tangle webs we weave! We did eventually get back together a few months later, but the same **cycle of pain** came up each time.

Apparently, when we separated for those few months, he contacted a former girlfriend and she took him in. I was quick to put my men out, because that is what I saw my mother do with my father. Now, of course, he told me that he had stayed somewhere else. The truth always comes out! Four months later, I was in the kitchen and I heard a knock at the Door. My husband was in the bathroom shaving and my youngest daughter was at the kitchen table doing her homework. When I opened my front door, a woman in her thirties, was standing with her hands on her hips! She said, "Oh, I see he decided to come back to you! This is when everything caught me by surprise and confused. I invited her in and immediately called for my husband to come out to the kitchen. Before I could get a word in, my husband immediately became defensive and belligerent towards the woman. He said, "Don't be coming by my house disrespecting my wife and my home.

Afterwards, I was so hurt and I felt humiliated. I just ran in my room closed the door and cried. My husband lied to me about his past living arrangements. The trust was lost and gone and I had a hard time getting it back. He apologized, and I tried to cope with it, but I could not. I became very insecure and once again reclusive. When this happened to me, I felt like I did when I was violated. It felt like my wounds had opened up again and were infected.

This was 2001, one year into the marriage and I had to go through this crap! I continued to put him out, thinking that, that was the answer. I put him out to escape the pain, but the pain never left. I asked him to leave and this time he found a room for rent!

But, I still did not trust him anymore, yet I loved him very much. That same year, my daughter Nicole gave birth to a beautiful baby girl. She named her Nia and she definitely brought some joy to my life! At first, I felt strange being a grandmother and now I would not change it for the world. My granddaughter calls me Mamma Leslie. "Isn't she beautiful?"

My Granddaughter, Nia

Also, another life changing event occurred, when my spouse and I decided to get back together after going to counseling in 2003. He moved back in the house during the month of January 2004.

Five months later, I decided to sell the house, which I regretted later on. The plan was to get a house together! During that year houses sold so fast and I got a buyer less than a week. I did not even get a chance to put the house on the market or place a sign on the front yard. Meanwhile, I had less than two months to find a place to live. The original plan was to rent an apartment in Owings Mills, MD for six months and then buy a bigger house by the end of the year. Well, time went by so fast and we found ourselves staying at the apartment for two years. At the end of the two years we both were at the end of our rope! The behavior started again! We treated each other so badly, that we each hated to come home. I never stayed out and neither did he, but we became very distant towards each other during the month of August 2005. I was so stressed at work and home and needed some emotional help. My brain was twisting and turning and I lost myself for a short while. I contacted a counselor and asked to be seen right away! The woman that I worked with was amazing and helped me discover my inner pains and hurts. When I first visited her, I wore dark sunglasses so that she would not see the sorrow in my eyes. As time went on, I felt very comfortable with her and decided to take off my glasses and look her directly in her eyes.

She helped me to open up to her and to be completely honest and not ashamed. I told her that I was depressed and she first asked me when the onset occurred. I initially told her that I felt overwhelmed at work and at home and that I did not feel like myself. I did not want to hurt myself, but I was not happy within. The day before I scheduled to see her, I had taken all the household pictures off the wall, pulled all my clothes out of the closet, and just screamed. I told her that I thought I had a mini break down. She was very patient with me while I explained my outburst to her. She asked me about the relationship with my spouse and my children.

She knew the right questions to ask and the right answers to give. She then decided to ask me questions about my childhood which I did not feel at the time was relevant to this case. The Counselor knew what I needed in order for me to move forward with my life. She had to find out about my past first and show me what the root of the problem was. I brought up everything about my childhood experiences, to my present adulthood experiences, so that I could try to put an end to this cycle of madness

I did not stay in counseling long enough to completely heal the wounds. It's very similar to not completing the antibiotic that the doctor prescribed to you to clear up an infection. When you stop taking your medicine just because the symptoms subside does not mean the infection is completely out of your system. Going to counseling is not just for attendance but wanting to receive a revelation and resolution for your problems.

The strange thing about my relationship with my spouse is that I didn't hate him, just his behavior. Unfortunately, we eventually dissolved our marriage. At this stage in my life, I needed to reexamine the situation and take a good look at my self and reevaluate the relationship based on my finding. I wished I had done that with my first marriage. I just did not know where all the hurt was coming from, until I revealed it to others.

Now, I will say that my second husband did not have his father in his life either. Not making excusing for him. But had I recognized the chances of us encountering problems, when the unit is not complete, then maybe I would have evaluated things a little differently. Both of my husband's fathers were not involved or present in their lives. My first spouse's father was an alcoholic and was physically abusive to his mother. The situation was totally opposite with my second spouse. His dad did not want anything to do with him since birth. Very similar to what I went through with Nicole's dad. Who thought that he did not have to play a role in nurturing her and did not accept her as his child? How painful that was for her and me! Of course, my second husband said that he was not affected by his father's absence in his life. Well, I do believe subconsciously he became bitter towards his father.

When we were married, the relationship was like a yoyo, because we gone back and forth with each other at least three-four times. He was not a fighter in the relationship, but he was a very angry man and at times was very abusive with his words or responses to me. He acted like he did not want the marriage anymore. So, we decided to split in March of 2006(3rd or 4th time). I have a hard time keeping track. By now my sister and my relatives are trying to understand why I kept going back to the same problems. My spouse and I never learned to identify the real issues, so we became very distant and unapproachable to each other.

Yes, I hated his behavior, not him, and I felt like I had to start the cycle all over again, by myself and without his support. So, I got involved with relationship a year later that I knew was not healthy for me. Yet I ignored the consequences, which only led to another **cycle of pain**.

I thought by meeting a different man it would ease the pain and that I could get him to love me for me. Since I did not feel love from my spouse. Well, that's all wrong.

You see, I had to learn how to love me for me. That's why it is so important to understand the importance of having self worth. Do you know that most of the time, the people you least expect are able to recognize your self worth even before you do. My friends use to always tell me how smart and bright I was and that I am a very assertive strong minded person. Yes, when it comes to my work or employment, I am fearless, but when it came to addressing my own inner feelings during that time, I was like a kitten.

As time has gone by, I have learned how to love, how to receive love, how to express love and how to forgive and how to let go, even when things appear to be so painful and impossible to understand. But before, I was an angry and bitter woman inside, which did not represent who God wanted me to be. I thank God for the discipline and correction he has done with me so far.

Learning how to allow myself to be molded by the creator has been a big challenge for me because I felt like I had the short end of the stick and I felt like I should not have to endure anymore suffering. Why me Lord? Why do I have to suffer? Why did I have to go through these **cycles of pain**? I started to find the answer through my suffering and my pain.

Pain- it is evitable, it is unpredictable, and it is a natural part of life experiences. You have to allow pain to go through its process, in order for your problems to heal. You can not interrupt the **cycle of pain** process through drinking, sexual activity, drugs, spending, socializing, or any other quick fix actions. Why? Well, pain is just like a cold. When you first experience the onset of a cold, your body lets you know that something is attacking your immune system and it initially starts off mild, but later on the cold starts to break you down and cause you to loose your natural ability to function. There's no quick cure for a cold. You have to let it take its course. The same applies to pain, you have to allow it to take its course and complete the cycle. If not, you will find yourself going through a continued cycle over and over again. Yes, pain hurts, whether it's physical or emotional. Most people do not like the way it feels. It is very uncomfortable and it can make you lose your mind if not treated properly.

However, when I started dating someone else, we both were still married and had not closed the book to the chapter before getting involved

I take full responsibility for my actions! I needed a male figure to talk to and I wanted to understand why men do what they do. I wanted to know why my past and present relationships always started off so well, but later became thorns in my side. However, I did discover that I had trust issues that I had not resolved. Once I was able to break some of the barriers of trust, I was able to move forward. You know the old saying Rome was not built in a day, so why do you think that you can change something in one day that took over your life for years.

Through continued self evaluation and reading I was able to piece together the issues that haunted and hindered me.

Trust is something that God has asked us to do for years. He tried to get us to trust him, but some of us have not yet opened our hearts completely to him. If you have a problem with trusting people, find out what the root of the problem is first, then learn how to forgive and you will win your life back. After reading an article from Imaculee Libagizza, she wrote about her personal tragedy during the Rwanda Massacre. I was astonished with the writer's words and thoughts.

She was one of the survivors of Rwanda who lost just about her entire family. The title of her article was "Forgiving the Unforgivable." She was a Tutsi and her family was murdered by the Hutu militants. She embraced what she called "Radical Forgiveness." Deciding to "drop all charges whether or not the person deserves to be forgiven" is what she stated. Her message was so powerful and after I read it, it caused me to look deep within my self and it helped me place that "Radical Forgiveness "in my heart. So, I hope that this message will become contagious not only for me, but for anyone who reads this book.

Before I decided to let go and let God, the male friend of mine offered me some value advice. He was like the brother I never had. He often told me that my (second) husband would not change his behavior until I changed mine. At first, I became a little defensive, because I felt as though I did nothing wrong.

He then proceeded to tell me how I needed to heal and not worry about why my spouse was not doing what he supposed to do. He said that I needed to learn how to make it all about myself for once. This was hard, because it had been a long time since I really got into myself like that. I had been bombarded with sexual abuse, parenthood, marriage, physical abuse, neglect and so much more at the same time. So, the habits were already ingrained and I became use to the stressful life that I was living. My friend did not approach me sexually although I knew there was a deep attraction between us. He was a great financial support for me during that time in my life. My spouse behavior towards me caused me to draw closer to my friend, who I fell in lust with. I felt like he had nurtured me back to emotional health.

He was 12 years younger than me and yes I felt like "Stellar Got Her Groove Back." I am so grateful for good genes, because when we were together, you could not tell there was a huge age gap between us. The very first time we became intimate is when, I stopped by to see him at his job. Every thought that I had was premeditated. I found myself wanting him and I had to have him, so when he cracked on my college sweat suit, I proceeded to take it off and show him what I had underneath. He looked at me with amazement and the rest is history.

He treated me like a lady and was very generous towards me. I could go on forever talking about his kindness, but that is not my main purpose for sharing this book with you. There is a lesson that I learned from all of my crisis and the moment's of joy! I began to want more and demand more, but during the entire time, I never looked in the mirror. Just like Michael Jackson used to sing, "The Man In The Mirror." Before you expect others to change, please take a look at yourself and examine yourself thoroughly. If you are holding on to any type of pain, bitterness, range or anger, let it go before trying to start a new relationship or change an existing one in your life.

So, I finally decided to change my behavior and not look for a man to define my purpose in life. God is my purpose, not my father, not my husband, and not the past relationships that I had. God is the strength and the joy of my life! So, all along I thought I could only be strong if I had my father in my life. For whatever reason, God knew that I could handle not having a father figure in my life and that's why God decided to lead me on a journey of discovery. This discovery took me places that I never imagined I would be and my journey required me to be placed in uncomfortable situations in order to tell you my story. Remember we all have a story to tell. So, stay on the path that God has placed you on.

MY DECISION TO COACH

That's why I decided to start a coaching practice that offers life coaching (5 Star Coaching Services, LLC). I want to reach individuals who have gone through some tough times, transitions, career changes, sudden changes, financial hardships, and who need some balance in their lives (especially for anyone who has been sexually assaulted). We all need to help each other or fail. Coaching is something I aspire to do the rest of my life. My main purpose is not about me, but about what God wants from me. He needs modern day disciples who aren't afraid to work for his glory. This life is not about how you perceive it, but how you will live it while you're able to be a blessing to someone despite your woes, your pain, and your disappointments.

Love will carry you through and according to I Corinthians 13:4-4 "Love is patient. Love is kind. It does not envy, it does not boast, it is not proud. It is not rude, it is not self-seeking, it is not easily angered, and it keeps no record of wrongs. Love does not delight in evil but rejoices with the truth. It always protects, always trusts, always hopes, and always perseveres."

A support group can help relieve some of the pressure and help guide you to a place of serenity. If we can't help each other grow, this world will self destruct. I am not saying to only surround yourself around things that have disrupted your life or your business. Learn to seek help before you fall down too far that your dreams and aspirations become paralyze. So, try to attack your issues just like an alcoholic does. You might need to go through a 12 step program of emotional, mental and spiritual healing.

The best medicine for your soul can be obtained by admitting your pain first. So, for your healing, I have created some steps that might help you cope with the cycles of pains in life.

12 INSPIRATIONAL KEYS FOR EMOTIONAL, MENTAL & SPIRITUAL HEALING AND HAPPINESS

Key #1

Learn How to Release Painful Situations
In Your Life

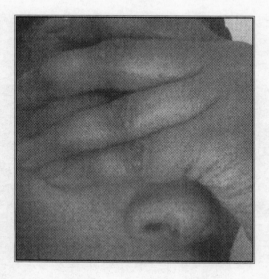

- Let other people who care about you, know about the pain you're feeling
- Discuss your problems with your pastor
- Reach out to family members, close friends and counselors
- Let go and let God

Key #2

Share Your Hurt and Pain With People That Are Supportive and Learn to Reciprocate

- Reach out to support groups pertaining to your need
- Form a support group with other people who have faced similar situations
- Become a vigilant healer for others

Key # 3

Write Down Your Hurt and Pain in a Journal

- There are benefits to expressing your pain in writing: It allows you to bring out what is bothering you and teaches you how to release your inner pain
- Writing is therapy for the soul and the mind
- Writing is simply your heartfelt words in action

Key # 4

Learn To Forgive the Unforgivable
(People That Have Caused you Pain)

- Forgiving empowers you
- Forgiving will heal your spirit and emotions
- Forgiving teaches others to change his/her behavior
- Forgiving is what God requires from all of us

Key #5

Accept Your Uniqueness and Different Way of Life

- God created each and everyone of us uniquely
- Use the gifts and talents that are instilled in you
- Don't live your life trying to impress others, rather learn how to impress and embrace yourself
- Don't compare yourself to others: the way you look, talk, smile, and laugh are all unique gifts from God

Key #6

**Focus On The Things That Will Help You.
Stay Away From The Things That Will Destroy
You Mentally And Emotionally.**

- Discover your passion and your gifts
- Keep your eye on God
- Learn to embrace your life
- Try to avoid dysfunctional relationships and friendships

Key #7

Pray and Meditate Daily

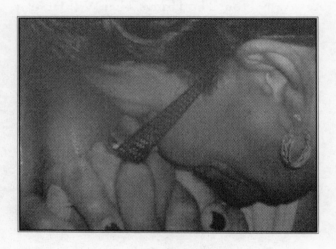

- Pray without ceasing
- Ask God for his daily bread
- Allow God's presence to dwell in you
- Meditate and ask God to help you with self- improvement

Key #8

Don't Allow Negativism to Control Your Life

- Treat negativism with a long handle spoon
- Worrying or negative thinking doe not add a single hour to your life
- Stay away from negative influences
- Don't allow a negative environment to become a dictator of your life

Key # 9

Find A Place to Relax & Think When Things Are Going Chaotic In Your Life

- Listening to the sound of running water can be soothing and relaxing
- Try taking a daily walk
- Discover places where you've never been before
- Get a full body massage
- Take a mini vacation as often as you can
- Sign up for a yoga, dance & meditation class

Key #10

Take Care of your temple

- Eat a nutritious meal daily
- Exercise as often as possible
- Avoid anything in excess
- Avoid anything that controls your body negatively
- Go to the doctors regularly

Key #11

**Live The Life That You Love
and
Love The Life That You Live**

- Be an outrageous dreamer
- Don't fear the impossible
- You are what you think
- Let the inner you come out

Key #12

TRUST IN THE LORD

With all your heart and lean not on your own understanding, in all
your ways acknowledge him, and he will make your paths straight.
Proverbs 3:5-6

LIFE EXPERIENCE
COACHING ADVICE

Family Coaching Advice:

Raising your children as a single parent:

Don't fret if you are the only parent that shows your child/children love. It all starts with you first. Show your children that you are more than a conqueror and encourage them to forgive even if the circumstances appear to be unforgivable. Just learn how to appreciate the life that you have. Believe me if anybody knows how hard it is to raise children alone, I am included in the statistics. However, I must profess that my mother did an outstanding job, with nurturing, loving and caring for my sisters and me. By watching her, I was able to model after her strength to pull through the adversity of parenthood. Sure there will be disagreements among your children and you will encounter all types of unexpected trials, but I guarantee you if you provide them with the Agape love, and raise your children to be close; they will be inseparable when they get older.

How to Live and Let Go:

We do not have the option to pick the types of parents that we have, but we do have the option to decide the type of life that we will accept. A life full of bitterness and anger is not healthy, so let go and live. Over the years I had finally learned how to love the life that God has given me, despite the chaotic life that I had endured. Life is what you make it, so make it count!

Overcoming feelings of abandonment:

Some families take neglect and abandonment so lightly, until they start having issues that they can't handle. It is so crucial to make sure that everybody in the family gets the proper love, care and attention, otherwise he or she can be easily influenced to go in the wrong direction. When God brought us in this world, He did not leave us comfortless. So, why do we leave our families members comfortless, when problems occur? Why is it so hard to sacrifice some time to pay attention to each other during the bad times as well as the good times? There is no reason why we should have our family members or friends living in the street or in a social rut. We all have an anchor that we can throw towards them if we get out of self.

However, sometimes we turn our backs on the people we should love and we develop a self-centered attitude and selfish heart. This attitude can cause some deep rooted pain and the pain can snowball into resentment and anger. If you have a difficult family member that seems to be draining you, still let them know how much you love them, regardless of their problems. Yet, still be stern and firm with them, but don't ever turn your back on anyone you say you love.

Sadness

Is a feeling that we all have to encounter and believe it or not, it is a grieving process that will allow us to heal and go to the next stage. God never promised us that we would not experience sadness, but he has reassured us that he would never leave us nor forsake us. So, consider sadness as a positive emotion that allows us to grow, overcome, persevere and come to terms with our feeling of sadness.

Feelings are like strongholds

Feelings are emotional, mental and physical. Starting with emotional feelings, whenever someone lets us down or disappoints us, we create a wall of destruction for ourselves. We shut down, and have a hard time trusting others again. This creates a stronghold and causes us to fall deeper and deeper into despair. Just remember feeling come and go. So, don't allow what you're currently feeling to dictate the rest of your life. Where is your faith?

- Try sitting down in a quiet place and breathe in and out slowly. (Now, don't you feel better already?)
- Focus on the positive aspects of your life and how much you look forward to getting back to that way of life.
- Try asking yourself these questions:
  Ask yourself – Why am I so sad? What can I do to get through this feeling of sadness or despair? Will I be sad forever? Is there anything too hard for God? Does a storm last forever?
- Over time you will be able to address your feelings directly and the negative thoughts will slowly dissipate.

Mental Strongholds

Mental strongholds are just as bad because when you allow things and circumstances to control your mind, you can fall into a catatonic state. You brain starts to shut down and you become lifeless. So, don't allow things to control your mind, beware of how you react to negative energy, people or outcomes. If you find yourself in a foggy and lifeless state, seek help right away.

Physical Strongholds

Evidence of physical strongholds is very easy to detect. When the body craves for immorality, everything you can imagine will have you surrendering to it. If its sex, you will become a slave to it. If its food you will over indulge with it. If its alcohol, you will thirst for it, and if its drugs you will yearn for it. So, don't allow your temple to become a prisoner to any of these bad habits. Most of the time, you are trying to fill a void that you never resolved.

- Pray without ceasing, because this stronghold can grab you like a pitbull's bite
- When you start to experience this stronghold, remove yourself from the influences that can cause you to regress
- Pay close attention to the negative energy or company around you
- Stop pretending that you have this stronghold under control. You will eventually be in denial of this stronghold, if you continue to feed its cravings

DEVOTIONAL MESSAGES

The Reasons Why I Love My Mother
By:
Daughter: Kelly Brunson

Words of Wisdom

How to Handle a Crisis
Who Jesus Is To Me
Happiness and Joy
What is Love?
Where is Your Faith?
A Breath of Fresh Air
What is Your Gift?
By:
Leslie Parker

The Reasons Why I Love My Mother!

I love my mother because she took responsibility in taking care of me
I love my mother because she taught me to achieve and be all that I can be
I love my mother because she is my friend, provider, and my shoulder
to lean on
I love my mother because she stood by me ever since I was born
I love my mother because she is someone who won't bend
I love my mother because she doesn't give up and I know she will win
I love my mother because she is someone special in the whole world
I love my mother because she loosens up and doesn't stay curled
I love my mother because she shows that she has a caring heart
I love my mother because she cares for her daughters and never leaves
them apart
I love my mother because she is my guardian angel till this day
I love my mother because she is thoughtful in every single way
These are the reasons why I love my mother, because she is everything
I ever wanted
That without having her I would be nothing!

I Love You,
Written by: Kelly (my daughter)

Words Of Wisdom

How to Handle a Crisis?

C- Create a plan of action
R- Revitalize yourself & your thoughts
I- Increase your ability to seek help
S- Search for support & programs that can help you recover
I- Invent or create ways to overcome the obstacles in front of you
S-Strengthen your mind, your emotions and your attitude

Who Jesus is To Me!

He promised me **J-oy** when my heart is aching.

He promised me **E-ternity** for repenting my sins.

He promised me **S-alvation** for believing in him and acknowledging that he died for me

He promised me **U-nity** as long as I stay on a straight and narrow path

Most of all he **S-acrificed his life** for me
(He paid a price He didn't owe and I owed a price I could not pay: Oh! What a mighty God we serve)

Happiness and Joy

Is your happiness based on what you possess? Does the world and the things of the world measure your happiness? Happiness is priceless and so is the Joy of the Lord. You cannot create it or manufacture it. If you really want true happiness, get out of self and allow God's love to dwell inside you!

What is Love?

L- Letting
O- Others
V- Value
E- Everything God has created you for!

Love is an action word, so don't allow meaningless things in your life. Remember God is the creator of Love and His Love surpasses all types of love. His love is real and unconditional. His Love will never change!

Where is Your Faith?

Is your faith with man, your family, your job, your friends, yourself or your imaginary hope?
There is only one real hope and faith! Have you figured it out yet? The hope I'm referring to is everlasting and true. It will give you the secret to living a life of purpose. "Trust in the Lord" and eliminate the imitations of life!

A Breath of Fresh Air

What does it feel like to breath in fresh air? Isn't it refreshing when you do?
When it flows through your body, does it feel like your insides have just been detailed and cleaned!
So, don't allow the debris of depression, oppression, despair, hatred, malice, jealousy, bitterness and hopelessness take residence in your soul. Learn to appreciate the fresh air that was first put in your body at birth! Breathe the breath of life!

What is Your Gift?

The Gift that God has given you is yours to keep as long as you share it with others. Don't hide it, don't ignore, don't forget it. Your gift is unique because it was given to you while you were in your mother's womb. So, treasure the special gift that God has given you:

G-od's
   I-nternal
      F-avor and
         T-reasure

Now you know how special you are! Share your gift and be proud of who you are and what you are able to do ☺

SUMMATION

This book is written to give men, women & children an opportunity to release whatever pain they have experienced over the years. We all have buried pain in our minds over the years and we each have unconsciously learned how to repress it. However, when we do this we develop anger, bitterness, rage and an unforgiving heart. The heart is where we hold our emotions and over time this will give us an emotional heart condition. This heart condition has been passed down to every generation. Women have become angry with the men in their lives, including their fathers, mates and brothers. Men have also become angry with the women in their lives, their mothers, mates and sisters, and children are angry with their parents, their siblings and even their peers. As you see, the cycle goes on and on. This book expounds on how I learned to turn the pain around and count it all joy. I know that it is a peculiar statement to make, but It will help you develop a mindset to survive and thrive. By all means, this is not a quick fix book, but it can give you an insight to heal and a will to persevere.

Sure sometimes it take years to recover from painful events, but when you do, you will become empowered and vigilant about helping others. So why not help stop the **cycle of pain** within your own family and other families. We all have various **cycles of pain**, but I believe we can overcome the pain with unconditional love. So, please join me with this quest in healing others who are broken. Again, I pray that this book will move you to go outside your comfort zone and move you to continually pray without ceasing.

NOSTALGIC PHOTOS

My parent's wedding pictures: Married at my
father's parents' home & my father's brother
Uncle Robert Lee was the best man

Picture Was Taken in 1957

My Mother's High School Portrait

Year: 1957

Grandfather and His Sisters

Childhood Photo of My sisters and I

From left to right: Dawn, Leslie, and Tammy
Year: 1963

Photo of My Mother, Her Simblings and My Grandmother Rena

From left to right: Aunt Syl, mother Clarice, my Aunt Rena and my Aunt Martha

Childhood Places Where I Lived

Lived here from the age of 6-8

Lived here from the age of 8-15

ABOUT THE AUTHOR

Leslie Parker is from Baltimore, MD and is the youngest of three girls. She attended Morgan State University and Majored in Telecommunication (Directing for Television) and later on decided to transfer to Towson State University in Towson, MD to complete her B.S. Degree in Mass Communication.

She has over 20 years experience in marketing and management and enjoys working with people. She has two beautiful daughters, and is blessed to have two beautiful grandchildren as well.

She was raised by a single mother and a host of other relatives who influenced her to pursue her passion in so many ways. Her inspiration to love others came from God, her mother, her grandmother, her aunts, her sisters, her children and a host of close friends.

Leslie is gifted and talented in all aspects of life. She is full of zeal, she loves to motivate people and encourage others who have gone through some difficult times in their lives. God has blessed Leslie with the gift to encourage, console and give advice.

She has always had a passion to help others, especially since she was a victim herself of sexual, physical and emotional abuse. Her unique ability to get strangers to open up to her and win their trust is part of her personality and gift. She has been able to provide great supportive skills to anyone who has experience trauma in their lives. Leslie has made a personal commitment to God to fulfil his purpose for her life.

Her desire to write and coach started when her friends, family members, former co-workers, and strangers, asked her for advice on personal issues.

Last but not least, she has a diverse work background which includes: Print and Radio Advertising, Ad Copy, Project Management and Real Estate. She is also the President and Founder of 5 Star Coaching Services, LLC (Support Group that provides individual and business coaching advice). For speaking engagements or coaching sessions, she can be reached via email or phone:

Leslie Parker
5 Star Coaching Services, LLC
5starcoachingsvcs@gmail.com
(410) 504-4695

www.5starcoachingsvcs.vpweb.com